W9-BLU-300

Who discovered Poland?
(see page 13)

What do you call a vampire from Tijuana?
(see page 32)

What's a Jewish mother's dilemma?
(see page 41)

What glows and can't scream?
(see page 55)

What's the definition of a loser?
(see page 86)

What's the ultimate in punk?
(see page 104)

Blanche Knott's
Truly Tasteless Jokes VII

ST. MARTIN'S PRESS/NEW YORK

To Mondo Condo

TRULY TASTELESS JOKES VII

Copyright © 1987 by Blanche Knott

Library of Congress Catalog Card Number: 87-50347

ISBN: 0-312-90765-6   Can. ISBN: 0-312-90766-4

Printed in the United States of America

First St. Martin's Press mass market edition/September 1987

10 9 8 7 6 5 4 3 2 1

CHERNOBYL

Did you hear about the hooker from Kiev?
  She gives glow jobs.

•

There's a new soup in the Soviet Union . . .
  Leek.

•

The Soviets are claiming discovery of a new element—
  Ukranium.

•

What's the weather in Kiev?
  Cloudy, with a high of about four thousand degrees.

•

Did you know the Ukraine used to be the breadbasket of Russia?
   Now it's the melting pot.

•

Have you seen the new Russian currency?
   It's called rubbles.

•

How can you recognize a Swedish baby born nine months after the Chernobyl disaster?
   Look for the blonde eyes and blue hair.

•

What has feathers and glows in the dark?
   Chicken Kiev.

•

How do you cook Chicken Kiev Chernobyl style?
   First, preheat the oven to 8,000 degrees . . .

•

And what do you serve with it?
   Black Russians.

•

Hear what the five-day forecast in Russia is?
   Three days.

•

General Motors is doing its part to help the survivors of the Chernobyl catastrophe.
   They're hiring them as headlights on their new 1987 models.

THE *CHALLENGER*

What does NASA stand for?
  Need Another Seven Astronauts.

•

What was the last thing Christa MacAuliffe said to her husband?
  "You feed the dogs, honey; I'll feed the fish."

•

What's the Space Shuttle Cocktail?
  7UP and a splash of Teacher's.

•

What color were Christa MacAuliffe's eyes?
  Blew. One blew left and one blew right.

•

Where did the astronauts spend their last vacation?
  All over Florida.

·

What subject did Christa MacAuliffe teach?
  Social studies . . . but now she's history.

·

When's the next space shuttle launch?
  The Fourth of July.

·

Did you hear the space program has a new official drink?
  They've switched from Tang to Ocean Spray.

·

What were Christa MacAuliffe's last words?
  "What's this button for?"

·

What was the last thing to go through Commander Francis Scobee's mind when the *Challenger* exploded?
  The control panel.

·

What did Christa MacAuliffe leave for her class when she joined the shuttle program?
  A blown-up picture of herself.

·

What was the last transmission received from the space shuttle?
    "No! Bud Light!!"

                    •

Why can't you send a teacher into space?
    She'll go to pieces.

                    •

Hear about the *Challenger* cocktail?
    Just one is powerful enough to blow seven people away.

                    •

Have you seen the new Transformers toy?
    It's a space shuttle that turns into a Ford Pinto.

                    •

Why do the NASA executives drink Sprite?
    They couldn't get 7Up.

                    •

What do you say to someone who's been offered a ride on the next shuttle?
    "Are you going to take the plunge?"

                    •

They have a new Shuttle Simulator software package out . . .
    When you press "Control B," it blows up.

                    •

Did you know that Christa MacAuliffe had dandruff?
   They found her Head & Shoulders.

•

What were *really* Christa MacAuliffe's last words?
   "Mind if I smoke?"

•

What do Tylenol, an old male walrus, and NASA have in common?
   They're all looking for a tight seal.

•

How many astronauts can you fit in a Honda Civic?
   Two in the front seat, three in the back, and seven in the ashtray.

•

What was the last meal served on the *Challenger*?
   Shake 'n Bake.

•

Christa MacAuliffe wanted to shower on board, you know . . .
   But then she decided to wash up on shore.

•

Why was there only one black aboard the *Challenger*?
   They didn't know it was going to explode.

•

What does the bumper sticker on Christa MacAuliffe's car say?
"I'd rather be teaching."

•

Why did she make such a bad teacher?
Because she blew up in front of her class.

•

Did you hear about her new book?
Around the World in Eighty Pieces.

•

What's the difference between the Patriots and the *Challenger*?
The Patriots made it past Miami.

•

What do the Patriots and the *Challenger* have in common?
They were both blown away within the first seventy seconds.

•

What was the weather forecast for January 28, 1986?
Light shuttles all day long.

•

What's worse than finding glass in your baby food?
Finding astronaut in your tuna fish.

•

How did Reagan open his speech on the day of the *Challenger* disaster?

"Well, I hope you all enjoyed the fireworks this morning."

•

Did you hear that NASA is looking for a new shuttle pilot with a burning desire to fry a spaceship?

•

What was the teacher's first lesson from space going to be about?

Spontaneous combustion.

•

Where should the crew of the *Challenger* end up?

In NASA's Hall of Flame.

•

What did the head of NASA say after reading the headlines?

"I wish they wouldn't blow this thing out of proportion."

•

If the astronauts' remains had been found, what would have been the best way for their country to serve them?

With coleslaw and french fries.

•

Did you hear NASA thought they'd come across a piece of the black astronaut?

It turned out to be the radiator hose from a '57 Chevy.

•

What did the astronauts say after the explosion?
"That was one hell of a blow job!"

•

Did you hear they succeeded in recovering most of the astronauts' body parts?
They're only three feet away!

POLISH

Did you hear about the tragic war between the Poles and the Germans?

The Poles threw dynamite, and the Germans lit it and threw it back.

•

Or about the two Poles that drowned in the back of a pickup truck when it went off the road into a river?

They couldn't get the tailgate open.

•

Or about the Polish musicians who had to stop playing from time to time to empty the saliva out of their instruments?

They were a string quartet.

•

Two Polish men found themselves sharing a jail cell and struck up a conversation. "I'm in for assault and battery," said one. "What about you?"

"Barnyard rape," answered the second man.

"Barnyard rape! What the hell's that?" asked his cell-mate.

"Well . . . I fucked a pig and it squealed on me."

•

Did you know Polish law has a "grandfather clause"?

It reads: "If your grandfather had children, you may have them too."

•

A man died and went to Heaven. At the pearly gates, as with all new arrivals, he was greeted by St. Peter and taken on a grand tour.

One particular chamber aroused the new arrival's curiosity. It housed an infinite number of clocks, each bearing someone's name, and every once in a while one would go around and chime.

In answer to the man's question, St. Peter explained that the clocks went around once every time someone in Heaven jacked off.

The new arrival happened to be something of an expert on surnames. "Can you tell me, St. Peter," he then asked, "why there are no Polish names on any of these clocks?"

"Oh, we have plenty of those but we keep them in the basement," St. Peter replied. "We use them as fans."

•

What does it say on the bottom of a Coke bottle in Poland?

"Open other end."

•

How about on the top of a Polish ladder?
   "STOP!"

·

Stanley and Ania got married and wanted desperately to make love and have a baby, but being Polish, they had never been taught how to "do it." So Stanley finally sought the services of Poland's greatest sex therapist, a Dr. Shenkowski.

Sitting the young man down in his office, Dr. Shenkowski said grandly, "Stanley, making love is one of the finest things that can take place between a man and a woman in marriage . . ."

"I know, Doctor, but could you please tell me exactly how to go about it?" interrupted Stanley, embarrassed but determined.

"Okay . . . well . . . uh . . . you, as a man, take the longest thing on your body and stick it into the hairiest part of hers," stammered the doctor and quickly showed him out.

Two months later a pissed-off Stanley walked back into his office. "Dr. Shenkowski," he yelled, "I've been following your instructions every night and Ania's still not pregnant. And frankly, I don't think this sex business is all it's cracked up to be! Some doctor you are."

"Now Stanley," said Dr. Shenkowski soothingly, "calm down and tell me exactly what went on between you two and maybe I can sort things out."

"Don't try and blame it on me," blustered Stanley. "I followed your directions to the letter. Every night I stuck my nose as far as it would go into her armpit."

·

Who discovered Poland?
   The Roto-rooter man.

·

How do they make Polish sausage?
From retarded pigs.

•

If you were comparing two pairs of contact lenses, how would you know which one belonged to a Pole?
His initials would be in the corners.

•

Why are Polish mothers so strong?
From raising dumbbells.

•

A carload of Polish friends came across the scene of an accident. "Oh my God," gasped the driver, pulling over for a closer look at the crumpled sedan, "that looks like Joe's car." So they all piled out and walked closer.

"Look," said the second, "that's Joe's arm—I'd know that watch anywhere."

"I'm sure that's Joe's leg," said the third, pointing out where it lay against the curb.

"And look—that's definitely Joe's head," shouted the fourth, running after an object rolling slowly down the street. "Joe, Joe," he cried, picking it up. "Are you all right?"

•

Did you hear about the Pole who was so stupid the other Poles noticed?

•

The Polish man was standing in the entrance to the downtown Hilton without a stitch on when a policeman grabbed him by the elbow. Hustling him towards the paddywagon, the cop said roughly, "As soon as we get some clothes on you, you're going down to the station, pal."

"But wait, officer, please," protested the young man, "I'm waiting for—"

"I don't care if you're waiting for the Queen of England," interrupted the cop, "you can't stand here naked as a jay-bird."

"But, officer, I'm waiting for my girlfriend. See, we were up in our room and she said, 'Let's get undressed and go to town,' and I guess I beat her downstairs."

•

How many Poles does it take to take a bath?

Six. One to lie in the tub and five to spit on him.

•

Three high-school pals were walking down the boardwalk when they came across the gorgeous girl in a string bikini. Two of the guys let out wolf whistles and stared their eyes out, but the third, who happened to be Polish, took to his heels in the opposite direction.

A few days later all three were walking down the boardwalk again and came across the same girl, this time wearing nothing but the bikini bottom. And again, two of the guys went ape while the Polish fellow ran for his life.

So when the guys saw the girl a third time—this time she was stark naked—two of them grabbed the Pole before he could get away. Shaking him by the shoulders, they shouted, "Why're you running away from a gorgeous sight like that, you jerk?"

Trembling, the Pole blurted, "See, it's like this: my mother told me if I ever looked at a naked woman I'd turn into stone . . . and I felt something getting hard."

•

A Pole and his friend were doing their business side by side in an outhouse. All of a sudden, the Pole jumped up, threw a dollar bill into the toilet, jumped after it, and started digging busily in the shit.

"What are you *doing,* man?" asked his friend.

"I dropped a quarter in by mistake."

"So why the hell did you throw a dollar in there?"

"I figured as long as I had to go down there anyway," explained the Pole, "I might as well make it worth my while."

•

There was once a Pole who decided to take a trip, and on the train he happened to be seated next to a gorgeous woman. Mustering his courage, he asked what perfume she was wearing.

"Chanel Number Five," was the frosty response. "It costs thirty dollars a bottle."

Later in the trip the unfortunate Pole had a bad attack of gas, and was forced to cut a silent but repulsively stinky fart. The woman looked over and asked what he had on.

"Kidney beans," he answered. "Thirty-nine cents a can."

•

Early one morning, while his son was getting ready for his first day of school, a Polish father took him aside and proceeded to instruct him on the appropriate way to urinate: "Okay, son: one, unzip your pants. Two, take out your penis. Three, pull back the foreskin. Four, pee into the urinal. Five, shake your penis off. Six, push back your foreskin. And finally, replace your penis and zip your fly back up."

Later that day, the father received a call from his son's teacher. "What seems to be the problem?" he asked.

"Well," the teacher said somewhat perplexed, "it appears that your son doesn't want to leave the bathroom."

"Oh, really? What's he doing in there?"

"We're not sure. He just keeps repeating, 'Three-six, three-six.'"

•

What did the Polish mother say to her unwed, pregnant daughter?

"Look on the bright side, maybe it's not yours."

•

Hear about the Polish husband who gave his wife a wig for Christmas?

He heard she was getting balled at the office.

•

Jerzy and Latvia were bored one day and decided to go to the zoo and taunt the gorillas. As they made faces at the apes, they didn't notice that one of the animals was getting quite turned on by Latvia's tits. All of a sudden, the ape reached through the bars, grabbed ahold of Latvia's blouse, and pulled her into his cage.

"What should I do!?" she screamed at Jerzy as the gorilla tore her skirt off and started to sexually assault her.

"Tell 'em what you tell me all the time, that you have a headache," he shouted back.

•

Hear about the new love lubricant for Poles?

Chapstick.

•

Stan and Milos decided to go on a fishing trip but they needed some equipment, so they bought rods, reels, fishing tackle, wading boots, creels, and a barrel full of worms. They had to rent a car so they could get to the cabin they had reserved in an isolated part of the Canadian wilds, and they had to put money down on a motor boat if they were going to get to that special fishing spot where all the pike and bass were just waiting to be hooked. Not only did they spend a huge amount of money, they also had to drive twelve hours, seven of them on rocky back roads.

Not fifteen minutes after they had arrived at the cabin, they were on the lake trolling for a bite. Unfortunately, they didn't catch a thing.

"No problem," said Stan. "We'll have better luck tomorrow." But they finished up the second day with nothing. The same thing happened the third, fourth, and fifth days until finally, on their last day on the lake, Milos caught a small perch.

The drive home was far from joyful, and Stan summed up the vacation with a depressing thought. "You know what, Milos? That fucking fish you caught cost us about a thousand dollars."

"My God," Milos said in amazement, "it's a good thing we didn't catch any more!"

JEWISH

How does a JAP do it doggie-style?
First she takes her clothes off and then she makes her husband beg.

OR

The husband gets on all fours and she rolls over and plays dead.

•

Hear what the rabbi said about performing circumcisions?
"The job stinks, but I get a lot of tips."

•

What's the difference between a JAP and taxes?
Taxes suck.

•

One Sunday, an old Jewish man walks into a Catholic church and sits down in a confessional.

"Forgive me, Father, for I have sinned," he said humbly. "Yesterday afternoon a beautiful girl with gigantic breasts and a cute little tush valked into my delicatessen and started making nice to me. Vell, what can I tell you, I closed the store and for the next six hours I fucked her. I vas like a crazy man or something."

"Excuse me, Mr. Epstein," interrupted a perplexed priest. "but you're Jewish. Why are you telling me?"

"Telling *you*?" yelled old Epstein. "I'm telling everyone!"

•

Did you hear about the new Jewish Army doll for girls?
    It's called G.I. JAP.

•

Why was the JAP snorting Nutri-Sweet?
    She thought it was diet coke.

•

Schwartz was walking down the street when a prostitute came up to him and asked, "Looking for a good time, big boy?"

"How much?" replied the skeptical Schwartz.

"Fifty dollars, sweetie."

"How about I give you twenty dollars for a simple blow-job?" Schwartz countered.

"What are you trying to do," the hooker screeched, "Jew me down or something?"

•

What do you call a Japanese JAP?
    An Orienta.

•

Why don't Jews like to vacation on Fire Island?

Because everytime they bend over to pick up a quarter—WHAM!

.

A concerned husband came home after seeing the doctor and sheepishly told his wife that he had a bad case of gonorrhea. Perplexed and somewhat naive, Mrs. Goldfarb went straight to the dictionary and looked it up.

"Shemp," she announced triumphantly, "you have nothing to worry about. It says right here that 'gonorrhea' is an inflammation of the Gentiles!"

.

Why do Jews have such short necks?

[Say "I don't know" as you shrug your shoulders.]

.

One day Joel and Jaime were sitting near the shuffleboard court when Joel turned to Jaime and said, "This is the proudest day of my long life. Today my grandson graduated from medical school!"

"N.Y.U.?" asked Jaime.

"And vy not?" answered the indignant Joel.

BLACKS

What do you get when you cross an ape with a black?
  A monkey-shine.

·

What do you call a thousand blacks without parachutes jumping out of a plane?
  Asphalt.

·

What's the black version of a fortune cookie?
  A piece of cornbread with a food stamp in the middle.

·

We all know of the scholarship fund started by Richard Pryor and Michael Jackson called the Ignited Negro College Fund . . .

But did you know they were both awarded honorary degrees as extinguished alumni?

•

What do you call a black bodybuilder?
  A Schwartzenigger.

•

What do you call a black hooker?
  "Sister."

•

What do you call a retired black hooker?
  "Grandma."

•

Did you hear about the black hooker with herpes?
  She charged extra for the bumpy ride.

•

Three black kids are sitting on a street corner dreaming about the fancy cars parked in front of the whorehouse across the street. The first one says, "When I grow up, I'm going to get a silver Coupe de Ville like that one over there."

The second kid pipes up, "Well I'm going to have myself a red Trans Am just like that one over there."

"When *I* grow up," says the third kid, "I'm going to get a whole big patch of fuzz."

"What the hell you gonna do with a whole big patch of fuzz?" his friends ask, mystified.

He looks at them coolly and explains, "Well, my sister just has a little piece of fuzz, and she owns botha those cars."

•

Did you hear about the black politician who was asked what he would do with Red China?

He said he'd use a purple tablecloth.

●

The city of Baltimore was plagued by rats, and the Mayor was going out of his mind trying to get them exterminated. Nothing was working. One day a little man wearing a knapsack strode into the Mayor's mansion and said he could unconditionally guarantee to rid the city of rats—for $15,000. A bit sceptical, the Mayor agreed to pay a third up front and the rest when the job was done.

Whereupon the little man took a little green plastic rat out of his knapsack. Winding it up, he placed it on the floor, and within minutes rats were coming out of the woodwork and following the man and the plastic rat out the door. Within a matter of hours the entire rat population of Baltimore had joined the caravan, far beyond the city limits and safely into the countryside.

Impressed, the Mayor had the additional $10,000 waiting for the little man when he appeared in his office the next morning. "You did a fine job there," he boomed. Putting a conspiratorial arm around the man's shoulders, the Mayor whispered, "Say . . . do you have a little green plastic nigger in that bag?"

●

What's black, white, and red all over?

South Africa.

●

Did you hear about the new book of nursery rhymes for black children?

It's called *Motherfucker Goose*.

●

A bus driver in Tuskaloosa constantly had to put up with fights between his black passengers and his white ones as to who had the right to sit where. Finally he pulled the bus over, made everyone get off, and lectured them sternly. "From now on, there ain't gonna be no more fightin' 'bout who's better, black or white. From now on, you're all blue."

The passengers looked each other over sheepishly and repeated, "We're all blue. Right on—we're all the same."

"Good," said the driver. "Now, back on the bus—sky blue people in front, navy blue people in back."

•

Did you know there were five makes of American cars named for blacks?

The Falcoon, the Jiguar, the Cooneville, the Coontinental, and the Poontang.

•

What penalty is this in football? [Pucker up your lips so they stick out as far as possible.]

Too many blacks on the field.

•

What's it called when you're mugged by twenty blacks?

High blood pressure.

ETHNIC VARIEGATED

A nice Italian boy was raised by his very strict mama, who forced him to promise not to marry an American girl. "You cannot trust them," she lectured her son time after time. "They cannot cook, they are no good in bed, and they will call you names, names to insult you like dago, wop, guinea. You hear me, Tony?"

"Yes, Mama," said Tony obediently, but over the years he had learned to tune out her litany. Indeed, when he turned twenty-one he realized his mother's worst fears by marrying an American girl.

"Tony, Tony," she wailed, "you'll never be able to trust her—"

"No, Mama, you've got the Americans all wrong," interrupted her son. "Tania is a good cook, she's great in bed, and she only calls me a dago when I call her a nigger."

•

What's worse than a retarded Puerto Rican?
    An Ethiopian with a tapeworm.

•

It was just before a critical offensive, and the Polish troops were being issued their weapons. Lenski was last in line, and they handed out the last rifle to the man in front of him. Furious, Lenski shouted, "Hey, what about my gun?"

"Listen, bud," advised the munitions officer, "just keep your hands out in front of you as though you were holding one, and yell, 'Bang! Bang!'"

"You gotta be joking," blustered Lenski. "You must be trying to get me killed!"

"Trust me," said the officer, sending Lenski out into the field with a reassuring pat on the shoulder.

Pretty soon Lenski found himself in the thick of battle with a Russian infantryman advancing on him. Having little choice, he raised his hands, pointed at the soldier, and yelled, "Bang! Bang!" The Russian fell over, stone dead. This worked on about twenty Russians. Fired with confidence, Lenski returned to the munitions officer and asked about a bayonet.

"Oh, we're all out," said the officer apologetically, "but if you just point with your index finger and scream, 'Stab! Stab!' you'll get excellent results."

Out went Lenski into battle again, and soon he was surrounded by heaps of dead Russian soldiers. In fact, he thought he had wiped out the whole platoon, and was just taking a breather when he saw a giant Russian coming toward him. Strutting forward, Lenski shouted, "Bang! Bang!"

The Russian kept on coming.

"Stab! Stab!" cried Lenski.

The Russian kept on coming, right over Lenski, crushing him to a pulp. The last thing the unfortunate Pole heard was the Russian muttering, "Tank, tank, tank . . ."

•

Know why most Polish jokes are so short?

So Italians can understand them too.

•

What's a jock strap?

A Mexican slingshot.

•

What's so great about getting a blow job from an Ethiopian woman?

You know she'll drink every drop.

•

"I tell you, sir, this is a great country and I praise God that I came over," the Irishman was expounding to a new acquaintance. "Where else, I ask you, could it happen that you could do a hard day's work, then find yourself outside the gates, standing in the rain, waiting for the bus—"

"You call that great?" queried the man next to him at the bar.

"Ah, but wait now. A big black limousine pulls up and the boss opens the back door and says, 'It's a hell of a night to be out in the rain. Why don't you come in here and warm up?' And when you're inside, he says, 'That coat's awfully wet—let me buy you a new one, all right?' And after that he asks where you live and says, 'That's a long drive on a night like this, why not come to my house?' So he takes you to his big mansion and gives you a big meal and a few drinks and a warm bed for the night and a hot breakfast and a ride back to work. I tell you, this is a great country. It would never happen to me in Ireland."

"And it happened to you here?" asked his acquaintance sceptically.

"No. But it happened to my sister."

•

You know how American boats say "U.S.S." and British boats say "H.M.S."?

Well, Italian boats say "A.M.B." Know what that stands for?

"Atsa My Boat!"

•

Why don't WASP girls like gang bangs?

For one thing, the sex is icky; and then there're all those thank-you notes.

•

What do you call a rich, good-looking, industrious Mexican?

An Italian.

•

What's the difference between a monkey and an Italian?

The Italian has more fleas.

•

Hear about the Indian who drank four gallons of tea?

He was found dead the next morning in his teepee.

•

How many Ethiopians can you fit in a bathtub?

I don't know—they keep slipping down the drain.

•

What's the difference between a Jewish American Princess and an Italian American Princess?

With the Italian, the jewels are fake and the orgasms real.

•

What do Mexicans call Bartles & James wine cooler?
Dos Okies.

* * *

A Pole, a black, and a Frenchman died and went to hell, where the devil made them an offer. "If you can name ONE thing I can't do," he boasted, "I'll let you out of here."

"Put all the watermelons in the world right here," demanded the black, and was immediately buried in a mountain of melons.

"Can you get me all ze Moet Chandon in ze world?" asked the Frenchman. He drowned in a tidal wave of champagne.

"Ready for mine?" asked the Pole cheerfully.

"You bet," said the devil, hands on his hips.

"Here goes," said the Pole, cutting a giant fart. "Catch it and paint it green."

* * *

What do you call a man who's half Welsh and half Hungarian?
Well Hung.

* * *

What do you call an Ethiopian paratrooper?
Gone with the wind.

* * *

What's invisible and smells like dirt?
Ethiopian farts.

* * *

What do you call an Englishwoman having sex?
   A dead end.

•

Why does Paris have so many tree-lined boulevards?
   So the German Army can march in the shade.

•

Did you hear the new anthem of African Nationalism?
   "Hey, Hey, We're the Monkees!"

•

What do you call a vampire from Tijuana?
   Spicula.

•

What's the difference between an Irish mother and her daughter?
   About five dollars.

•

Why couldn't the Greek bob for apples?
   His sister was using the toilet.

•

Sergeant Mack had a fine time during his stay in Hong Kong, but paid for it when he came down with a strange Oriental venereal disease. So he made the rounds of every American doctor in the community. To his horror he discovered that not only were they unable to cure him, they all informed him that the only course of treatment was to have his penis amputated.

Desperate, Sergeant Mack made an appointment with a leading Chinese doctor, figuring that he might know more about an Eastern malady. "Do you, Doctor Cheung, think I need to have my dick amputated?" he asked anxiously.

"No, no, no," said the Chinese doctor testily.

A huge smile broke out over the serviceman's face. "Boy, that's *great*, Doc. Every one of those American medics said they'd have to cut it off."

"Those Western doctors—all they ever want to do is cut, cut, cut," explained Dr. Cheung exasperatedly. "You just wait two weeks. Penis fall off all by itself."

•

Did you hear about the Pakistani problem in Toronto?

Yeah; it's so bad they had to divide the city into three zones: Urban, Suburban, and Turban.

•

A prosperous Japanese businessman decided to visit England and had such a pleasant stay that he decided to return the following year. This time, though, it was his bad luck to hand over his 2000 yen to a particularly rude and harried clerk at the exchange desk in the airport.

Counting the money he had shoved through the grill, the Japanese protested in heavily accented English, "Last time I get two hundred British pounds. Now only one hundred forty."

"Fluctuations," said the clerk tersely, motioning to the next customer.

The indignant Japanese drew himself up to his full five feet and snapped, "Fuck you British too!"

•

Fred was the manager for a construction project in downtown Rochester and his first job was to take bids from the local construction companies for the job. The first interview was with a representative from Zabriskie Brothers.

"You've seen the plans," said Fred. "How much'll you charge to get the job done?"

"Two hundred thousand dollars," said the Pole.

"Reasonable," commented Fred. "What's the break-down?"

"One hundred thousand for materials, one hundred thousand for labor."

"Okay," said Fred, jotting down the bid and showing him to the door, "I'll get back to you."

The next interview was with Gennaro Rossellini of Fratelli Rossellini, who came up with a four-hundred-thousand-dollar bid. "Half for labor, half for materials," he explained.

"That's a little high," admitted Fred, "but I'll get back to you."

The third bid came in from Ben Cohen of Cohen Construction. Calculating quickly, he offered, "Six hundred thousand dollars."

"Jesus, that's high," exclaimed Fred. "Could you break that down for me?"

"You bet. Two hundred grand for me, two hundred grand for you, and two hundred grand for the Pole."

•

One day while they were walking home after work, Pasquale offered to buy Luigi a drink. Over beers at the local tavern, Pasquale leaned forward and asked in a stage whisper, "Luigi, you like women with hairy legs?"

"Hell no," answered Luigi, his nose wrinkling in distaste.

"How about women with the long black hair under their arms?"

"You think I like to fuck monkeys or something?" answered Luigi. "Thatsa not for me."

"How about when they got the hair in a bun and a big wart on the end of the nose?" pressed Pasquale.

"I tell you, I no like none of these things," returned his friend angrily.

"Then, Luigi," asked Pasquale, looking him straight in the eyes, "if you don' like none of these things, how come you fuckin' my wife?"

•

When Bridget complained to the doctor of severe intestinal pains, he told her he needed a sample. "And what does he mean by that?" she asked her husband over dinner that night.

"I wouldn't be knowing," admitted her husband. "You'd best ask Katherine."

Now Katherine had lived in Glasgow and was forever putting on airs about her worldliness, and Bridget hated asking her anything, but she didn't know who else to turn to. So off she went to Katherine's house, only to return half an hour later all battered and scratched.

"An' what happened to ye?" asked her startled husband.

"She tol' me to go pee in a bottle," reported Bridget, blushing scarlet, "so I told her to go shit in her hat."

•

Nothing was too good for the eminent Russian diplomat visiting Washington. In fact, the "red carpet" treatment even included the services of a fancy call girl.

After a single kiss, the Russian asked her, "Vere's de vool? Vere's de vool?"

"'Vool'?" repeated the puzzled prostitute. "Oh, I get it— we American women don't have mustaches like the girls at home."

Next she removed her blouse. But instead of admiring her bountiful breasts, the diplomat ran his hands under her arms and asked, "Vere's de vool?"

"We American women shave under our arms," she explained somewhat impatiently, going on to remove her skirt and stockings.

"Vere's de vool?" asked the Russian immediately after rubbing her legs. "Vere's de vool?"

"We American women shave our legs," said the hooker indignantly. "And by the way, what do you want to do— fuck, or knit a goddamn sweater?"

HOMOSEXUAL

What do you call a gay man who's had a vasectomy?
A seedless fruit.

•

Feeling romantic one day, Stan brought his lover home a beautiful bunch of roses, but they brought on a tremendous attack of sneezing and wheezing. "I didn't use to be allergic to roses," gasped Teddy, blowing his nose.

Stan was still feeling romantic the next day and came home with a beautiful bouquet of lilies, but they had the same effect. And when an armful of chrysanthemums sent Teddy straight to bed, Stan lost his temper. "This is ridiculous," he snapped. "You should see a doctor."

So Teddy made an appointment with a well-known allergist, bringing the suspect bouquets with him. After a series of tests, the doctor called Teddy into his office.

"What should I do, doctor?" asked Teddy. "We're desperate."

"Get your boyfriend to change florists," advised the allergist. "This one uses pussy willows in his arrangements."

•

What's a 71?
Sixty-nine with two fingers stuck up your ass.

•

What's the difference between Seattle and San Francisco?
Seattle has ferry terminals and San Francisco has terminal fairies.

•

How many fags does it take to mug a woman?
Five. Four to hold her down and one to do her hair.

•

Did you hear about the new hospital for fags only?
There're no doctors or nurses. Just aides.

•

What did the fag from Alabama say to his three friends?
"Y'all cum now."

•

Did you hear about the gay who said he wasn't sure about his homosexuality?
He was only half in earnest.

•

How about the homosexual who said he was also a necrophiliac?

He was in dead earnest.

•

A fag came into a bar on the rough side of town. He went right up to a burly truck driver and started making conversation, and five minutes later they walked out together.

The next day the fag limped into the same bar, all bandaged up and one leg in a cast.

"What happened?" asked the bartender.

So the fag explained that it went like this. "When we got to his place he fed me and undressed me and bathed me and dried me off and dressed me in this divine nightie. And then he picked me up in both arms and took me out on the balcony . . ." A dreamy look came over the gay man's face.

The curious bartender urged him on.

"Well," sighed the fag, "he asked me if I was his little blue bird. I said 'You bet.' And he said, 'So fly, little blue bird, fly!' and threw me off."

•

What do you call a gay Boy Scout?

A Wee-blo.

•

What do lesbians do for dinner?

They eat out.

•

Did you know the Statue of Liberty has AIDS?

They don't know if she got it from the mouth of the Hudson River or from the Staten Island Fairy.

•

What's the number of the AIDS hotline?
1-800-BUT-FUCK.

·

What do you call a Jewish lesbian?
A kike dyke.

·

A very effeminate gay man got all dolled up in his pink hat with the white fringe, pink-and-white ruffled shirt, white chaps and pink tooled boots, saddled up with his pink saddle, and rode over to the local bar. Sashaying up to the bar, he ordered a pink lady and looked around the empty room. "Say, cowboy," he trilled to the bartender, "where is everybody?"

The bartender answered, "Up on the hill hanging a queer."

·

What's vaseline?
Meat tenderizer.

·

Beset with grief, a poor homosexual had just found out that he had AIDS. "What am I going to do?" pleaded the man after his doctor had reviewed the symptoms.

"I think you should go to Mexico and live it up. Drink the water and eat all the Mexican cuisine you can get your hands on, including raw fruits and vegetables," advised the doctor.

"Oh, God, doc, will that cure me?" squealed the gay.

"Not really," answered the doctor, "but it will teach you what your asshole's for."

·

What's a bitter transsexual?
  One who bites off his nose to spite his face.

•

What's the definition of a gay masochist?
  A sucker for punishment.

•

What happened to the fag who butt-fucked an Eskimo?
  He got Kool-AIDS.

•

What do you call a faggot in a chariot?
  Ben-Him.

•

A homosexual gets some suppositories from his doctor, but he doesn't know how to insert them up his own asshole.

  "Before you get dressed in the morning," the doctor instructs, "stand on a mirror and bend over. You should have no problem."

  Before getting dressed the next morning, the fag takes his mirror down off the wall and stands on it. Suddenly, he gets a terrific boner. Chuckling, the fag looks at his penis and says, "It's just me, silly."

•

What's a Jewish mother's dilemma?
  Having a gay son who's dating a doctor.

•

A car runs into the rear of the car in front waiting at a stop light. A fag jumps out shrieking, "My car! Look what you did! I'm going to sue you for five thousand dollars!"

"Five thousand dollars!" yells the other driver in amazement. "All I did was dent your bumper a bit. You can kiss my ass!"

"Well, well," the fag smiles, "maybe we can settle out of court."

•

Two Polish gays enjoy a long night of buttfucking and cocksucking. As one of them is leaving the next morning, he puts out his hand to shake good-bye.

"What! Are you crazy?" admonishes the other fag. "I heard you can get AIDS that way!"

•

What do you call a group of faggot lions?
A gay pride.

•

What's an IUD for homosexuals?
A fruit loop.

•

A fag is wheeled into the emergency room and tells the doctor on duty, "My lover got a little upset and shoved my glasses up my ass. Is there anything you can do?"

The doctor feels around the fag's butt, softly prodding and probing while muttering, "Mmmm."

"Doc, tell me what you see," the fag begs.

"I don't see anything, young man," he admits.

"That's funny," the fag giggles, "I can see *you*."

•

Hear what the two gays did after their disagreement over who was going to wear the pink boa to the dance?

They exchanged blows.

•

A county sheriff picked up a fag from the big city after the residents of the sleepy little town complained that the homo was propositioning some of the local boys.

"Okay, you fruitcake," the sheriff said in disgust, "you got fifteen minutes to blow this town or I'll throw your queer ass in jail."

"Oh my," cooed the fag, "I'd better get started. I *love* a challenge."

•

Hear about the new form of Russian Roulette for homosexuals?

You pass around six boys; one of them has AIDS.

•

What does a gay nurse give his patients?

First-AIDS.

CELEBRITY

•

What did Len Bias and Rock Hudson have in common?
  They both got hold of some bad crack.

•

What new basketball league is being formed in honor of Len Bias?
  The Six Foot and Under League.

•

Why is Len Bias like a bunch of daisies?
  Two days after you pick them, they die.

•

What's black on the outside and white on the inside?
  Len Bias.

•

Did you hear about the results of the recent drug-testing conducted among professional athletes?
   They found that cocaine took the Bias out of sports.

●

What do you and Len Bias have in common?
   Neither one of you will ever play for the Celtics.

●

Who's the only Celtic under six feet?
   Len Bias.

●

Remember Donald Manes, the Queens Borough President who committed suicide in the face of the Parking Department scandal?

Know why I don't like playing golf with Donald Manes?
   He slices when he drives.

●

What did Donald Manes say to his wife when he went out that night?
   "Just going out for a few slices."

●

How come he made it back home?
   He avoided the major arteries.

●

How does Claus Von Bulow like his eggs?
   Sunny-side-up.

●

So how did Jim McMahon catch it?
  He stuck his meat in the refrigerator.

                              •

Remember Billie Jean King's sponsor, Snap-On Tools of America?
  Now they have a new jingle: "Good Vibrations!"

                              •

What does it mean to go on the Scarsdale diet?
  You shoot your doctor and then spend the rest of your life eating bread and water.

                              •

What did Robert Wagner say to his wife on the night of November 29, 1981?
  "Sure, Natalie, have another drink—just don't go overboard."

                              •

What's funnier than Richard Pryor Live?
  Andy Kaufman dead.

                              •

What do the Indianapolis Colts and Billy Graham have in common?
  Both can make 20,000 people stand up and yell "JESUS CHRIST!"

                              •

What did Henry VIII, Rock Hudson, and Donald Manes have in common?
  They all screwed Queens and died.

                              •

Know where Rock Hudson was born?
   Ohio, but he was reared in California.

.

What do Michael Jackson and the New York Yankees have in common?
   Both wear one glove for no apparent reason.

.

What's the definition of poetic justice?
   Jesse Helms with sickle-cell anemia . . . or Anita Bryant with AIDS.

.

Did you read the *Irish Times* headline the morning after Chappaquiddick?
   "God Saves Sen. Kennedy as Girl Drowns. Devout Pair Believed to Be on Their Way to Midnight Mass. Ted Prays for Nine Hours Before Leaving Accident Scene. Irish Govt. Blames Ital. Contractors for Faulty Bridge."

.

Why did Michael Jackson stop fucking girls?
   He ran out of rubbers and started using his gloves, but the rhinestones hurt.

.

What movie best describes Mick Jagger's girlfriend?
   Romancing the Stone.

.

Did you hear that Boy George was going *straight*?
   It was just a rumor.

.

How about the new rock group, Motley Jew?
Their albums are called "To Fast for Pennies" and "Shout at the Bagel."

•

What do you get when you cross Madonna and a migrant worker?
Someone who's always Crossing the Borderline.

•

What do you call a black vocalist in the electric chair?
Shock-a-con.

•

Why did Arnold Schwarzenegger and Maria Shriver marry?
They want to breed the first bulletproof Kennedy.

•

What's the difference between Madonna and Joan Collins?
Madonna is like a virgin.

•

What would you call Tina Turner if she danced on somebody's sex organs?
A Privates Dancer.

•

What did Bob Geldoff come down with?
Live AIDS.

•

Hear about the new porno movie starring Arnold Schwarzenegger?
  It's called *The Sperminator*.

•

Why did Indira Gandhi change her deodorant?
  Her Right Guard was killing her.

•

Why was there no Halloween in India last year?
  No Gandhi.

•

Why did they shoot Gandhi so many times?
  They were aiming for the dot.

•

Did you hear the Carnegie Deli named a sandwich after
Vanessa Williams?
  It's called "Tongue on a Brown Bun."

•

Or about the Vanessa Williams commemorative stamp?
  You lick it on both sides.

•

What were Baby Faye's last words?
  "You're not going to make a monkey out of me!"

•

Why does Joan Collins's diet consist mainly of salads?
  She eats like a rabbit too.

·

When did Boy George's mother suspect something was fishy about her son?
  When he was in high school, he asked to spend his junior year abroad.

·

The Mayflower Madam has decided to write a children's book. Know how it starts?
  "Once upon a time there were seven little prostitutes."

·

What did Nancy Reagan say when the press asked her about her sex life with the President?
  "Ever try to shoot pool with a rope?"

·

Jerry Falwell has such an enormous ego, he screams his own name when he comes.

·

Know why Renee Richards can't stand getting a flu shot?
  The last thing she wants is another prick.

·

What's the difference between Joan Collins and the *Titanic*?
  It took several tugs to get the *Titanic* out of her slip.

HANDICAPPED

Did you hear about the man engaged to a woman with a broken leg?
He broke it off.

•

How about the woman dating Siamese twins?
She was "Torn Between Two Lovers."

•

Or the man who divorced his wife because of illness?
He got sick of her.

•

A door-to-door vacuum-cleaner salesman was quite taken aback when a truly horrible-looking little boy, his face mangled and his body twisted, answered the doorbell. Appalled by his deformities, the salesman still managed to speak up.

"Good morning, young man, is your mom at home? I'd like to sell her a vacuum cleaner."

"She's in an institution," mumbled the boy, whose cleft palate kept him from speaking very clearly.

"I see," said the salesman, warming to his pitch. "Can I speak to your dad, then?"

"Nope. He's in an institution too."

"So how about I talk to your older brother, and maybe leave my calling card?" the salesman suggested hopefully.

"He's at Harvard," said the little boy patiently.

"Now, wait a minute," said the salesman after thinking this over. "Your mom and dad are both in institutions and—no offense—you don't look so hot yourself, but your brother's at *Harvard*? What's he doing there?"

"He's in a jar."

•

How do you make a Venetian blind?
  Poke him in the eye.

•

How do you get a dwarf to give you a blow-job?
  You tell her to go up on you.

•

Have you heard about the teacher who was fired for being cross-eyed?
  She couldn't control her pupils.

•

Why did Pepperidge Farm start making exploding cookies?
  Because Pepperidge Farm dismembers!

•

Why did Jerry's kids go to the Twisted Sister concert?
  They wanna walk!

.

How long can you live without a brain?
  How old are you?

.

How do you make a dead baby float?
  Take your foot off its head and let it rise to the surface.

.

What glows and can't scream?
  A wet baby with its fingers in an electrical outlet.

.

What do you get when you screw a Coke?
  Burpees.

.

Among many other attractions, the traveling circus featured
Wanda the Wondrous, a faith healer who claimed the ability
to heal any malady, slight or serious, real or imagined. She
usually drew a big crowd, from which she would select a few
people on whom to practice her healing skills. Among the
unfortunate one Friday night were Cecily Sussman, on
crutches due to a congenital spinal malformation, and Irving
Bland, who had suffered from a terrible lisp all his life.
"Cecily and Irving," asked Wanda, "do you wish to be
healed?"
  "Yeth, ma'am," said Irving, and Cecily nodded vig-
orously.
  Wanda motioned them behind a purple velvet curtain and
proceeded to chant and pray, grinding powders together and

swaying before the audience. Finally she intoned, "Cecily, throw out your left crutch."

A crutch came sailing over the curtain.

"Cecily, throw out your right crutch."

A second crutch clattered on the floor at the healer's feet.

"Now, Irving," asked Wanda solemnly, "say something to the people."

Irving's voice came clearly from behind the purple curtain. "Cecily Sussman just fell on her ass."

.

What did Baby Fay die of?
   Baboonic Plague.

.

What do you call a guy/girl with no arms or legs:
in your flower garden?
   Rose or Bud.
In a jewelry store?
   Ruby.
In court?
   Sue.
On stage?
   Mike.
On your Christmas tree?
   Holly.
Out in the sun?
   Ray.
In a whirlpool?
   Eddy.
In Congress?
   Bill.
In a salad bowl?
   Letitia.
And on your mantel?
   Buck.

.

Mrs. Jones began to get nervous when dark fell and her husband hadn't returned from his regular Saturday golf game. Dinnertime came and went and she became more and more anxious, so when she heard his car pull in, she rushed out to the driveway. "Where've you been? I've been worried sick!" she exclaimed.

"Harry had a heart attack on the third hole," her husband explained.

"Oh, no! That's terrible."

"You're telling me," moaned her husband. "All day long it was hit the ball, drag Harry, hit the ball, drag Harry . . ."

•

What did the midget say when the judge asked him to tell the court if he had a defense for the rape charge he'd been convicted of?

"Hey, Your Honor, it wasn't my fault, my friends put me up to it."

CRUELTY TO ANIMALS

If Tarzan and Jane were Puerto Rican, what would Cheetah be?

Pregnant.

•

How can you tell if an elephant is in the same dark room with you?

You can smell the peanuts on his breath.

•

A mouse met a giraffe and fell in love with her, and after much entreating on the mouse's part, the giraffe agreed to spend the night with him. So the mouse's best friend was surprised to run across him the next morning looking like hell. "What happened to you?" he asked.

"Between the kissing and the screwing," said the mouse wearily, "I must have run a hundred miles."

•

What should you look for when buying a one-ton canary?
  A psychiatrist.

•

How can you tell if there's an elephant under your bed?
  Your nose is touching the ceiling.

•

What's the result of a bomb blast in the middle of a herd of cows?
  Udder destruction.

•

What did one fly say to another?
  "Gee, time is fun when you're having flies."

•

An extremely well-endowed gentleman went into a whorehouse, but there was no one there who could handle him. He left one girl after another bleeding and yelping in pain, until the madam came to their rescue. "This looks like a job for Betty," she said, beckoning to the customer. "Down this way, fourth door on the left, and whatever you do, don't turn on the lights."

The man obeyed her instructions and had a pretty good time, even though he couldn't see her and all he could hear was heavy breathing. When at long last he was satisfied, he said suavely, "I had a pretty good time, Betty. How about you?"

And out of the darkness came a satisfied, "Moooo."

•

Did you hear about the pregnant bedbug?
It had a baby in the spring.

•

What do you give sick birds?
Tweetment.

•

How do you get down from an elephant?
You don't; you get down from a goose.

•

What should you do if you come upon an elephant?
Wipe it off.

•

Two rabbits hopped past each other in a field and one suddenly took a hard look at the other. "Pierre," he said, "ees that you?"

"Oui, oui, c'est moi, Papa!" cried the younger bunny. "It's been so long, and I have so much to tell you. I, Pierre, have become the greatest lover in all of Versailles. I line up the female bunnies in the field and—bang, bang, bang—I knock them all down."

"Oh, Pierre," said his Papa sadly, "how could a son of mine have so little savoir faire, not even to say 'bonjour' before, and 'merci' afterwards. You are not the greatest lover in Versailles. Tomorrow you line up the ladies, I will start at one end, you will start at the other, and we will see who can boast the most prowess."

So the next morning Pierre has about a dozen lovelies lined up when his father saunters over and says, "Eh bien, Pierre, I will start here." He starts in, "Bonjour . . . Merci . . . Bonjour . . . Merci . . . Bonjour . . ."

And from Pierre's end of the line is heard, "Bonjour . . .

Merci . . . Bonjour . . . Merci . . . BONJOUR—ooh, pardon, Papa . . ."
   "Ohh, Pierre, MERCI!"

●

What does a black parrot say?
   "Polly want a white woman?"

●

How many mice does it take to screw in a light bulb?
   Two—the trick is getting them in there.

●

Tommy was playing outside when an elephant came out of the trees and into his yard. The little boy had never been to the zoo and had no idea that an elephant had escaped the day before. Running back in the house, he yelled, "Mommy, Mommy, there's a big dog in the yard."
   "Is that so," she said. "Just where is this dog?"
   "In the vegetable garden," gasped Tommy, "pulling up carrots with his long tail."
   "Oh, really? And then what's he doing with them?"
   Tommy blushed. "Mom, you wouldn't believe it."

●

What do termites eat?
   Woody Woodpeckers.

●

Did you hear about the fly on the toilet seat?
   He got pissed off.

●

A pig went into a bar and asked what the limit was. "Ten drinks," answered the bartender.

"Gimme fifteen," snorted the pig, and the bartender set them up. No sooner had he guzzled them down than the pig asked where the bathroom was.

"Down the hall and on the left," answered the bartender, and the pig ran down the corridor.

Shortly thereafter a second pig sauntered into the bar, inquired about the limit, ordered twenty drinks and swigged them down, asked after the bathroom, and ran off down the hall. And he was followed by a third pig, who drank twenty-five drinks, and a fourth, who downed thirty.

So by the time the fifth pig came in, the bartender knew what to expect and set up thirty-five drinks. The pig drank them down and just sat there on his stool.

"Well," asked the bartender, "aren't you going to ask where the bathroom is?"

"Nope," said the pig. "I'm the one that goes wee-wee-wee-wee all the way home."

•

What's the difference between a man and a bird?
A man doesn't eat with his pecker.

•

What do you call a rabbit with fleas all over him?
Bugs Bunny.

•

What's a Spanish Human?
An insecticide that makes flies so horny they screw themselves to death.

•

What does a dog do that a man steps into?

Pants.

•

Warren worked for a small mining operation so he was used to the desolate little towns of the Southwest. But when he was sent to Dry Gulch for a couple of months, something seemed strange from the very beginning, and one night in the local saloon he realized what it was. "Say," he said to the bartender, "aren't there any women in this town?"

"Nope," admitted the bartender. "The men here had so little to offer that all the women packed up and left years ago."

Warren's face fell. "That's pretty grim. What do the guys do on a Saturday night?"

"They do it with pigs," was the bartender's cool reply.

"Yecch!" Warren retched and left in disgust. But after a few weeks of total boredom he found himself back in the saloon, and casually inquired as to where the pigs in question were to be found.

The bartender was free with the information. "Just behind the farmhouse at the top of the hill."

One look at the pigs slopping around in the muddy pen was almost enough to send Warren back down the hill. But just as he was turning away, he spotted the cutest pig you could ever hope to see, with big brown eyes, a bow on the top of her head, and not a bit of mud on her little pink trotters. Quite smitten, he led her out of the sty, down the hill, and into the saloon for a drink. But to Warren's surprise his arrival caused quite a commotion, and all the seedy types backed away from him into the far corners of the bar. "Hey, what's up?" asked Warren angrily of the bartender. "You told me everyone in the place goes out with pigs."

"True enough," admitted the bartender, "but we weren't expecting you to take the *sheriff*'s girl."

•

A woman hitchhiker on a lonely country road was delighted to see a truck with a trailerful of chickens barreling towards her. Sure enough the eighteen-wheeler came to a stop, and when she opened the cab door she was greeted by a burly fellow and his parrot.

"Hey, little lady," said the driver leaning over towards the girl. "What can I do for you?"

"Can you give me a ride?" she asked demurely.

"Sure thing, little lady, but you're going to have to fuck me first."

"No way!" protested the hitchhiker. "I don't need a ride that badly!"

"NO FUCK, NO RIDE!" he screamed as he yanked the passenger door shut and zoomed off down the road.

Shortly after this incident took place, the parrot—who had been quiet throughout the exchange with the hitchhiker—started to repeat over and over, "NO FUCK, NO RIDE! NO FUCK, NO RIDE!" Finally the driver yelled, "Say that one more time, you idiot bird, and I'll throw you back with the chickens!"

Not two seconds had gone by before the parrot screamed, "NO FUCK, NO RIDE!" The driver slammed on the brakes, grabbed the parrot by the neck, and tossed it in the back with all the fowls.

Two miles down the road, the man saw the flashing lights of a patrol car in his rear view mirror and pulled off to the side. "But officer, I wasn't going that fast," the trucker began to protest.

"That's not the problem, sir," the policeman responded. "I pulled you over to tell you that you've got a parrot back there throwing chickens out the trailer, shouting, 'NO FUCK, NO RIDE!'"

•

Mary had a little lamb . . .
    . . . That'll teach her to stay out of the barn.

•

What's a ram-rod?
   A goat's hard-on.

·

A man with a frog perched on top of his head goes to see a doctor.
   "What seems to be the problem?" the physician asks.
   "My ass," the frog responds, to the amazement of the doctor.
   "And . . . uh . . . what's wrong with your ass?" the doctor inquires further, somewhat nonplussed.
   "Would you believe," complains the frog, "this started as a wart?"

·

One afternoon a farmer was telling his neighbor how to screw a sheep. "The trick," he shared with his friend, "is to sneak up behind her, grab ahold of her rear legs, spread 'em and lift 'em up to your dick."
   "That sounds easy enough," the other farmer said, "but how do you kiss her?"

·

What is Woody Woodpecker's girlfriend's name?
   Suzie Splintercunt.

·

What is a female dog's best friend?
   A bone-r.

·

Hear about the dog that could track anything? Well, it belonged to old Silas, an avid fisherman. One time he snagged a pair of lace panties some girl had tossed in the creek, and after the dog got a good whiff, why he led Silas to the biggest school of trout you ever did see.

•

A devout Catholic and his parrot hailed a cab and asked the driver to take them to church. "Are you bullshitting me?" was the cabbie's response.

The irritated passenger assured him that that was his destination. "And please don't curse," he added, "or my parrot will repeat your foul language."

They started off down the road and soon the driver opened his window and said, "Dig the fucking breeze."

"Please shut up," demanded the passenger. "I don't want my parrot to hear such things."

So the taxi neared the church, hitting the curb as it rounded a corner. "Shit, I hit the curb," cursed the cabbie, at which the passenger jumped out with his parrot, opting to walk the rest of the way.

He made it in time for Mass, where the priest was telling the congregation that everyone should learn to love one another. "Are you bullshitting me?" squawked the parrot. Mortified, his owner jumped to his feet and threw the parrot out the nearest window.

"Dig the fuckin' breeze," said the bird dreamily, who had never bothered to learn to fly. "Oh shit, the fucking curb . . ."

•

A man went into a bar one evening and ordered a beer. But no sooner had the bartender set it in front of him than a little monkey appeared from nowhere, perched on the rim of his glass, and promptly dunked his balls in the man's beer.

Enraged, the patron ordered another beer, but again the monkey was too fast for him. And when it happened with his *third* beer, the man really lost his temper. "Bartender," he yelled, "can't you do something about this goddamn monkey?"

"I'm sorry, sir, but you'll have to take it up with the piano player," suggested the bartender. "It's his monkey."

So the guy went over, leaned into the piano player's face, and said, "Listen, buddy, do you know your monkey's dunking his balls in my beer?"

"Don't think I do," answered the pianist, "but if you hum a few bars, I'll try and fake it."

FEMALE ANATOMY

What do you get when you cross a stripper and a fruit?
  A banana that peels itself.

•

How about when you cross an elephant and a prostitute?
  A hooker who does it for peanuts and won't ever forget you.

•

What does a cow have four of and a woman have two of?
  Feet.

•

A young couple hadn't been married for long when, one morning, the man came up behind his wife as she got out of the shower and grabbed her by the buttocks. "Y'know, honey," he said smugly, "if you firmed these up a little bit, you wouldn't have to keep using your girdle."

Her feelings were so hurt that she refused to speak to him for the rest of the day.

Only a week later he again stepped into the bathroom just as she was drying off from her shower. Grabbing both breasts, he said, "Y'know, honey, if you firmed these up a bit, you wouldn't have to keep wearing a bra."

The young wife was infuriated, but had to wait till the next morning to exact her revenge. Waiting till her husband stepped out of the shower, she grabbed him by the penis and hissed, "Y'know, honey, if you firmed this up a little bit, I wouldn't have to keep using your brother."

•

What does a woman say after her third orgasm?

You mean you don't know?

•

You know God wouldn't have made women smell like fish . . .

. . . if He hadn't made come look like tartar sauce.

•

An elegant woman swathed in furs entered a very expensive pharmacy in her neighborhood. Coming up to a white-gowned employee, she asked him where batteries for her vibrator could be located.

The young man thought for a moment, then turned towards the rear of the store, saying politely, "Come with me."

"If I could come that way," spat the dowager, "I wouldn't need the batteries."

•

How can you tell if a girl is ticklish?

Give her a test-tickle.

•

My new girlfriend is a witch: last night we were driving along when she put her hand on my knee—and I immediately turned into a motel.

•

About a month ago the President of the United States decided he had to get laid. Going to a high-class whorehouse, he found a blonde, a redhead, and a brunette waiting in the downstairs lounge. "I'm the President of the United States," he said to the blonde. "How much will it cost me to spend a little time with you?"

"Three hundred dollars," was her answer.

To the redhead he posed the same question.

She replied, "Five hundred dollars."

He made the same proposition to the brunette.

She replied, "Mr. President, if you can raise my skirt as high as my taxes, lower my panties as far as my wages, get your dick as hard as the times, keep it hard for as long as I have to wait in line at the store, keep me warmer than my apartment in the winter, and screw me like you do the public, believe me, Mr. President, it isn't going to cost you a dime."

•

"The man next to me is jerking off!" hissed Irene to her girlfriend as they sat in the darkened movie theater.

"Just ignore him" was her friend's advice.

"I can't," moaned Irene. "He's using my hand."

•

What happens when a girl puts her panties on backwards?
  She gets her ass chewed out.

•

Did you hear about the girl so dumb that when someone blew in her bra she said, "Thanks for the refill"?

•

The young lady was wearing an extremely tight skirt, and when she tried to board the Fifth Avenue bus she found she couldn't lift her leg high enough to reach the step. She reached back to undo her zipper a bit, but it didn't seem to do any good, so she reached back and unzipped it again.

Suddenly the man behind her lifted her up and put her on the top step.

"How dare you!" she demanded, turning to face him.

"Well, lady," he replied, "by the time you unzipped my fly for the second time I figured we were good friends."

•

What do you call two women in the freezer?
  Cold cunts.

•

What's the smallest cemetery in the world?
  The vagina—it only takes one stiff at a time.

•

What's the definition of an overbite?
  When you're eating pussy and it takes like shit.

•

What do you give a robot who's having her period?
  An S.O.S. pad.

•

Why is 68 the speed limit for a woman in bed?
  Because at 69 she blows a rod.

•

A woman goes into a bar and sits down. The bartender asks what she'd like to drink and she says, "Bring me a beer."
  "Anheiser Busch?" asks the bartender.
  "Just fine, thanks," she answers, "and how's your cock?"

•

What the difference between pussy and cunt?
  A pussy is soft, warm, inviting . . . and a cunt is the person who owns it.

•

Why don't girls drink beer on the beach?
  They might get sand in their Schlitz.

•

What do a woman and a stamp have in common?
  You can lick 'em, stick 'em, and send 'em away.

•

What's the ultimate in embarrassment for a woman?
  When her Ben-Wa balls set off the metal detector at the airport.

•

What's the definition of a cunt?
A root canal.

•

Three friends go to the grand opening of a new bar, and after a couple of beers one asks the bartender why the place has no name. "Just couldn't come up with one I liked," he answered, and offered free beers to anybody who comes up with a good one.

"How about 'Jack's Place'?" suggested the first guy, but the bartender said it was too common.

"'Lucy's Place'?" proposed the second guy. The bartender turned that down too, but when the third guy came up with "Lucy's Legs," he enthusiastically agreed. The winner was served his free beers, but when he arrived the next day, the bar was closed. After fifteen minutes a cruising cop car pulled up and the policeman asked why he was sitting there.

The guy answered, "I'm waiting for Lucy's Legs to open so I can get a free drink."

•

"Say," said Lucille one day over lunch, "weren't you going to go out with that guy who played the French horn?"

"Yeah," said Diane, stirring her ice tea.

"You were really looking forward to it, I remember. How'd it go?" Lucille leaned forward eagerly.

"Actually he was a pretty nice guy," volunteered Diane reluctantly. "But there was one real problem . . ."

"Oh, really?"

"Every time he kissed me, he wanted to shove his fist up my ass."

•

What did the Florida entrepreneur name his whorehouse?
Bush Gardens.

•

What's another reason God created the orgasm?

Because he couldn't wait for the second coming.

•

A certain couple fell on really hard times, and since the husband already worked full-time and part of a night shift, they decided the only way to keep the family afloat was for the wife to go out and sell herself.

One night she went out and didn't return until the wee hours, disheveled and exhausted. Watching her flop onto the sofa like a limp dishrag, her husband said sympathetically, "You look like you've really had a rough night, honey."

"I sure have," she gasped.

"Well, did you make a lot of money at least?" he asked.

His wife managed a proud smile. "One hundred and thirty dollars and twenty-five cents."

"Twenty-five cents!" exclaimed the husband. "Who was the cheap bastard who only gave you two bits?"

"Why," said the woman, "*all* of them."

•

Why did the hooker wear French heels?

She didn't want to sell herself short.

•

"That was . . . terrific. Really amazing!" gasped the new boyfriend gratefully.

"I'm glad you liked it," said the girl demurely. "I learned it in the circus."

"No kidding? How's that?"

"I was a sword swallower."

•

The newlyweds undressed and got into bed. "Sweetheart," asked the new wife, "could you please hand me that jar of Vaseline over there."

"Baby, you aren't going to need any Vaseline," he growled amorously. But at her insistence he handed it over, and she proceeded to smear it liberally all over her crotch.

After watching this procedure, the husband asked the wife a favor. "Remember that long string of pearls I gave you for an engagement present? Could you get them out of the bureau drawer for me?"

"Of course, lover," replied his bride, "but whatever do you want them for?"

"Well," he explained, looking down at the Vaseline smeared all over her, "if you think I'm going into a mess like that without chains, you're crazy!"

•

"Can you see that?" asked the optometrist of his lady patient, pointing at the last line of his chart.

"No."

"How about this line?" The optometrist moved his pointer upward.

"Can't make out a thing."

"Now?" The pointer was aimed at the huge letters on the top line.

"Nope."

The optometrist opened his fly, pulled out his dick, and said, "Lady, can you see THIS?"

"Oh yes," she replied, tittering.

"I thought so—you're cockeyed."

•

"I do happen to need somebody," admitted the owner of the hardware store to the unimpressive-looking man who was interested in a job. "But tell me, can you sell?"

"Of course," was the confident reply.

"I mean really *sell*," reiterated the shopkeeper.

"You bet," said the young man.

"I'll show you what I mean," said the owner, going over to a customer who had just walked in and asked for grass seed. "We're having a very special sale on lawn mowers," he told the customer. "Could I interest you in one?"

"What do I need a lawn mower for?" protested the customer. "I don't even have any grass yet."

"Maybe not," said the owner agreeably, "but all that seed's going to grow like crazy some day and then you'll need a lawn mower in the worst way. And you won't find them on sale in midsummer, that's for sure."

"I guess you've got a point," admitted the fellow. "Okay, I'll take a lawn mower too."

"Think you can do that?" asked the storekeeper of his new employee after he'd written up the bill. The man nodded. "Okay, good. Now I have to run to the bank. I'll only be gone for a few minutes, but while I'm gone I want you to sell, sell, sell."

The new guy's first customer was a woman who came over and asked where the tampons were.

"Third aisle over, middle of the second shelf."

When she came to the counter to pay, he leaned over and said, "Hey, you wanna buy a lawn mower? They're on sale."

"Why on earth would I want a lawn mower?" she asked, eyeing him suspiciously.

"Well, you aren't going to be fucking," he blurted, "so you might as well mow the lawn."

•

With one look at his voluptuous new patient, all the gynecologist's professional ethics went right out the window. Instructing her to undress completely, he began to stroke the soft skin of her inner thigh. "Do you know what I'm doing?" he asked softly.

"Checking for any dermatological abnormalities, right?"

"Right," crooned the doctor, beginning to fondle her breasts and gently pinch her nipples. "And now?"

"Looking for any lumps that might be cancerous."

"Right you are," reassured the doctor, placing her feet in the stirrups, pulling out his cock, and entering her. "And do you know what I'm doing now?"

"Yup," she said, looking down. "Catching herpes."

MALE

Joe was in the corner bar having a few when his friend Phil dropped in and joined him. It didn't take long for Phil to notice a string hanging out of the back of Joe's shirt collar that his friend kept tugging on.

Finally Phil couldn't contain his curiosity, and asked "What the hell's that string for?"

"Two weeks ago I had a date with that dish, Linda," Joe explained, "and when I got her into the sack, would you believe I couldn't perform? Made me so mad that I tied this string on it, and every time I think of how it let me down, I pull the string and make it kiss my ass."

•

Marvin liked to hang out at the beach, and he couldn't help noticing this other guy who had girls all around him like bees around a flower. Finally Marvin went over to shoot the bull with the lifeguard. "Some guys have all the luck, eh?" he commented. "Just look at that one; you just know he's getting more pussy than any man can handle. How come I'm not making out like him?"

79

"You really want to know?" said the lifeguard with a grin. "The next time you come down to the beach, try putting a potato in your bathing suit."

This sounded like a good suggestion to Marvin, so he couldn't understand why everyone was cracking up when he took his next stroll in the surf. "Hey, man, I just followed your advice," he complained to the lifeguard. "How come everyone's laughing at me?"

The lifeguard leaned forward and whispered confidentially, "The potato's supposed to go in the *front* of your suit."

•

What did one ball say to the other?

"Why should we hang? It was Peter that did all the shooting."

•

A young couple was parked on Lovers Lane and the young man turned admiringly to his pretty date and said, "Gee, you smell good. You wearing perfume or something?"

The girl blushed charmingly and confessed that she was wearing a new perfume that she'd bought especially with him in mind. "You smell good too," she said. "What do you have on?"

"Well, I have a hard on," blurted the young man, "but I didn't know you could smell it."

•

A couple of truck drivers met at a diner on an interstate. "Yo, Jack," said one to the other, "I haven't seen you in months. How're you doing? Getting any on the side?"

Jack sighed wearily and said, "I haven't had any in so long I didn't know they'd moved it."

•

Hey there, have you ever read the print at the bottom of a condom?

No? Oh, I see . . . you never had to unroll it that far.

•

Why's a tight pair of pants like a small hotel?

There's no ball room.

•

A woman had a big old German Shepherd that snored so loudly she could never hear her soap operas in the afternoon. Over coffee one morning she happened to mention the problem to her neighbor, who leaned over and whispered confidentially that she had just the solution. "The next time it happens, tie a ribbon around his balls and he'll stop," said the neighbor. "He won't even wake up."

That afternoon, during the first few minutes of *As the World Turns,* the dog came in and flopped down in front of the TV. Within three minutes he had flopped onto his back and begun snoring deeply, so the woman ran to her sewing room and grabbed a red ribbon. Sure enough, the neighbor was right: when the ribbon was tied around his nuts the dog stopped snoring, and never even woke up.

That very night was her husband's bowling night, and he came home very late and very drunk. He fell into bed, rolled onto his back, and began to snore loudly, and as his wife lay there sleepless she thought again about her neighbor's suggestion. Fetching a blue ribbon from her sewing box, she tied it around her husband's balls. He fell silent and never stirred.

Later on that night the husband woke up to take a leak. Still pretty drunk, he staggered down the hall, let the dog out, and went to pee. Looking down at his cock, he noticed the blue ribbon, and when he let the dog back in, he noticed the red one. "Woofer," he said blurrily, "I don't know where we've been . . . but at least we came in first and second."

•

81

Why do men swim faster than women?
   Because they have a rudder.

•

What do you call a two-hundred-foot-long rubber?
   A condominium.

•

What's the definition of a macho?
   Someone who's been circumcised with pinking shears.

•

What do you call a man with no dick?
   A sucker.

•

How about a mountain climber who's had a vasectomy?
   Dry sack on the rocks.

•

Who's the most popular guy at the nudist camp?
   The one who can carry two cups of coffee and a dozen doughnuts at the same time.

•

Heard about the new generic rubbers?
   They're for cheap fuckers.

•

An assembly-line worker became increasingly obsessed with his desire to stick his penis into the pickle slicer. Finally, worried that he'd be unable to contain the desire, he finally sought the advice of a psychiatrist.

"You know, I had a case not unlike this one a few months ago," said Dr. Bernstein, thoughtfully rubbing his beard, "a man who kept wanting to put his hand on a hot stove."

"So what happened?" asked the factory worker.

"He went ahead and did it," confessed the doctor, "and he burned himself, but he never had the desire again. So my advice is to go ahead and follow your impulse in order to free yourself."

"Okay, doc." And the patient left.

At his next appointment the doctor asked what had happened.

"I took your advice," said the man, "and stuck my penis into the pickle slicer."

"So then what happened?" asked the psychiatrist, leaning forward eagerly.

"We both got fired."

•

What's six inches long that every woman loves?
   Folding money.

•

Edith and Roberta were hanging out their laundry in their back yards when the talk came around to why Marcia's laundry never got rained on. So when Marcia came out with her laundry basket, Roberta asked her how come she always seemed to know in advance whether it was going to rain. "Your laundry's never hanging out on those days," she commented in an aggrieved tone.

Marcia leaned over her fence and winked at her two friends. "When I wake up in the morning I look over at Buddy," she explained. "If his penis is hanging over his right leg, I know it's going to be fair weather and I come right out with my laundry. On the other hand, if it's hanging left, for sure it's going to rain so I hang it up inside."

"Well, smarty-pants," said Edith, "what's the forecast if Buddy's got a hard-on?"

"Honey," replied Marcia with a smile, "on a day like *that* you don't do the *laundry*."

•

An eight-year-old boy was charged with the rape of a grown woman, and though the charge seemed highly unlikely, the state's evidence was overwhelming. As a last, desperate move, the defense counsel came over to his client on the witness stand, pulled down his pants, and grabbed the little boy's tiny penis. "Ladies and gentlemen," the lawyer cried, gesturing toward the jury box, "surely you cannot believe that such a small, as yet undeveloped organ is sexually mature?" Growing more agitated, he went on, "How could it be capable even of erection, let alone the rape of a twenty-eight-year-old—"

"WATCH IT!" yelped the kid from the stand. "One more shake and you'll lose the case."

•

A man was experiencing chronic infections so he took his urologist's advice and entered the hospital for a routine circumcision. When he came to, he was perturbed to see a large group of doctors standing around his hospital bed. "What's up, doc?" he asked nervously.

"Uh, well . . . there's been a bit of a mix-up," admitted his surgeon. "I'm afraid that instead of a circumcision, we performed a sex-change operation on you. You now have a very nice vagina instead of a penis."

"What!" gasped the patient. "You mean I'll never experience another erection?"

"Oh, I'm sure you *will*," reassured the doctor, "only it'll be somebody else's."

•

If a man's case of VD is called herpes, what's it called when his wife catches it?

Hispes.

•

Who should you see if your hand isn't enough?

A wet nurse.

•

A man once explained to me that his penis was four inches. "Now some women like it," he went on, "but others complain it's just too wide."

•

Hungry for company, the young couple is delighted when a spaceship lands on their very isolated farm and out steps a young, very humanoid, Martian couple. They get to talking and soon the wife invites the Martians to dinner. And over dinner the conversation is so stimulating and all four get along so well that they decide to swap partners for the night.

The farmer's wife and the male Martian get the master bedroom, and when he undresses she sees that his phallus is very small indeed. "What are you going to do with that?" she can't resist asking.

"Watch," he says smartly. He twists his right ear and his penis suddenly grows to eighteen inches in length—but it's still as skinny as a pencil. And again the farmer's wife can't suppress a disparaging comment. So the Martian twists his left ear, at which his prick grows thick as a sausage. And he and the woman proceed to screw like crazy all night long.

The next morning the Martian couple takes off after cordial farewells, and the farmer turns to his wife. "So how was it?" he asks curiously.

"It was fabulous, really out of this world," reports the wife with a big smile. "How about you?"

"Nothing special," admitted the farmer. "Kinda weird in fact. All night long she kept playing with my ears."

•

What do you call sperm from a reporter?
Journaljism.

•

Two men were standing at adjacent urinals when one said to the other, "I'll bet you were born in Newark, Ohio."

"Why, that's right," said the second man in surprise.

"And I'll bet you were circumcised when you were three days old."

"Right again. But how'd you—"

"And I'll bet it was done by old Doc Steadman."

"Well, yes, but how did you know?" asked the second man in amazement.

"Well, old Doc always cut them at a sixty-degree angle," explained the first guy, "and you're pissing on my shoe."

•

What's the definition of a loser?
Someone a hooker tells, "Not now—I have a headache."

•

When Mike came into the office for the results of some medical tests, the doctor told him he had some good news and some bad news. Mike asked for the good news first.

"Your penis is going to grow two inches in length and an inch in circumference."

"That's terrific," Mike exclaimed, breaking into a big smile. "So what could be bad?"

The doctor answered, "Malignant."

•

What's the big risk with electric blankets?
  Wet dreams.

•

The customer came up to the pharmacist indignantly. "Last Friday I ordered twelve dozen rubbers," he said angrily, "and when I got home I found I'd been shorted a dozen."
  "Gee," said the pharmacist, "I hope I didn't ruin your weekend."

•

When is it justified for a woman to spit in a man's face?
  When his mustache is on fire.

•

Jim is having an affair with his boss's wife, and one afternoon they're going at it when they hear footsteps on the stairs. "Quick," hisses his lover, "jump out the window."
  Fortunately, it's a first-floor apartment and even more fortunately, the New York City Marathon happens to be passing by, so Jim just falls into step with the pack.
  "Tell me something," gasps the man running next to him, "do you always wear a condom when you run?"
  Thinking fast, Jim replies, "Only when it looks like rain."

OLD AGE

How do you know when you're getting old?

When your wife gives up sex for Lent and you don't find out till Easter.

•

Two old men meet while tottering around the park on their morning constitutional. "Irving, how are you?" asks one, patting his friend on the arm.

"Terrible, terrible," mutters Irving. "Memory's going. For instance, I can't remember whether it was you or your brother who died."

•

Why did the undertaker serve Coke at his grandmother's funeral?

Because Coke adds life.

•

The old couple sat through the porno movie twice, not getting up to leave until the theater was closing for the night. "You folks must have really enjoyed the show," commented the usher on the way out.

"It was revolting," retorted the old lady.

"Disgusting," added her husband.

"Then why did you sit through it twice?" asked the puzzled usher.

"We had to wait until you turned up the house lights," explained the old woman. "We couldn't find my underpants, and his teeth were in them."

•

What's the difference between an old woman and an old man?

Wrinkled boobs.

•

What do women and dogshit have in common?

The older they get, the easier they are to pick up.

•

A young woman was walking toward the bus stop when she came across a little old man sitting on the curb, sobbing his heart out. Moved by his grief, the woman bent over and asked him what was so terribly wrong.

"Well, you see," choked the old man, "I used to be married to this awful bitch. She was fat and ugly, never put out, the house was a pigsty, and she spent my money like water. She wasn't even a decent cook. My life was hell."

His listener clucked sympathetically.

"Then she died," sobbed the old man, "and I met this beautiful woman. Twenty-eight years old, a body like Sophia Loren and face like an angel, a fabulous cook and housekeeper, the hottest thing in bed you could possibly imagine, and—can you believe it?—crazy over me! She couldn't wait to marry me, and treats me like a prince in my own home."

"This doesn't sound so bad," volunteered the young woman.

"I tell you, I'm the luckiest man in the world." The old coot bent over in a racking spasm, convulsed with sorrow.

"Well, then," said the woman tentatively, "what's to be so unhappy about? Why are you sobbing on the street corner?"

"Because," he sobbed, "I can't remember where I live!"

•

One day, while walking down a deserted street, an old bag lady was accosted by a determined thief. "I'm telling you the truth, I don't have any money," she pleaded, but the mugger wouldn't believe her and started to feel around her bra for a possible hiding place.

"Young man," she cooed, "I told you I don't have any money—but if you keep that up, I'll write you a check."

•

An elderly nymphomaniac walked into a bar with a pigeon on her head and shouted, "Whoever can guess the weight of this bird can fuck me!"

Way in the back of the bar, a drunk yelled, "One thousand pounds!"

"Close enough," the whore answered cheerfully.

•

Peter and James have been life-long friends for over sixty years. One day Peter says, "James, let's make a pact: whoever dies first will try to come back and tell the other what heaven's like."

They both agree, but none too soon, because the next day James is done in by a sudden heart attack. Six months later, just when Peter is giving up any hope of hearing from his friend, a voice wakes him up in the middle of the night.

"James, is that you?" Peter asks in amazement.

"You're right, you're not wrong," James answers.

"Well, tell me. What's it like?"

"You wouldn't believe it. All day long, all we do is eat and fuck. We get up in the morning, eat breakfast and fuck, then we eat lunch and fuck until dinner. After dinner we fuck some more. We fuck until we pass out then we wake up and fuck some more," James explains.

"Holy shit!" exclaims Peter. "If that's heaven, I can't wait to die!"

"Who said anything about heaven?" a perplexed James replies. "I'm in Nevada and I'm a rabbit."

•

"The doctor said I have the legs of a seventeen-year-old!" announced the old woman triumphantly to her husband.

"Big deal," her husband chuckled sarcastically, "what did he say about your sixty-five-year-old ass?"

"Oh," she replied, "he didn't mention you."

•

"Things sure ain't the way they used to be in the old days," the old woman said to her granddaughter.

"How's that, Grandma?" asked the inquisitive little girl.

"Back then, the postman *always* came twice."

•

"Excuse me, doctor," asked the nurse, "but why is that old man sticking out his tongue and holding up his middle finger?"

"That's simple enough, nurse," answered the doctor, "I asked him to show me his sexual organs."

•

"Doctor, I'm losing my sex urge," complained Ruth at her annual checkup.

"Mrs. Beeston, that's understandable at eighty-four," said the doctor, "but tell me: when did you first start noticing this?"

"Last night," she answered, "and then again this morning."

"Aha," said the doctor. "Your problem isn't a diminished sex drive, it's that you're not getting enough. You should be having sex at least fifteen times a month."

Thanking him and heading home, the old woman couldn't wait to report the doctor's prescription to her husband. "Guess what, Pop? He says I need it fifteen times a month!"

Pop put in his teeth and said, "That's just great, honey. Put me down for five."

•

Herschel was astounded—and a little worried—when Reuben announced his upcoming marriage to a twenty-year-old girl. "At your advanced age," cautioned his friend, "couldn't that be fatal?"

Reuben shrugged philosophically. "If she dies, she dies."

•

What is the first warning sign of old age?

When you've been in bed all night with a woman and the dawn comes, but you haven't.

RELIGIOUS

A priest walked past a little boy sitting on the sidewalk with a bottle of kerosene. "What's in the bottle, my son?" asked the priest gently.

"Miracle liquid," was the boy's answer.

"Oh no, my son," corrected the priest. "The only miracle liquid is holy water. Did you know that if you rub it on a pregnant woman's belly she'll pass a baby?"

"That's nothing, pop," said the kid. "If you rub this on a cat's ass, it'll pass a motorcycle!"

•

Wanting to raise money for his parish, and having heard that people made fortunes in horse racing, a preacher decided to buy a racehorse. The prices at the local auctions were so steep, however, that the preacher ended up buying a donkey instead. And then, since he owned the animal, he decided he might as well go ahead and enter it in the races. Much to his surprise, the donkey came in third in its first race.

The next day the racing form carried the headline: "PREACHER'S ASS SHOWS."

The preacher was so pleased with the donkey that he entered it in the races again. This time the donkey won, and the racing form headline read: PREACHER'S ASS OUT IN FRONT.

The bishop had made no comment at the first headline, but the second bit of publicity upset him so much that he forbade the preacher to enter the donkey in any more races. The next day, the form read: "BISHOP SCRATCHES PREACHER'S ASS."

This was too much for the bishop, and he ordered the preacher to get rid of the animal. Chagrined but obedient, the preacher decided to donate it to a nearby convent. Next day's headline read: "NUN HAS BEST ASS IN TOWN."

The bishop fainted. When he came to, he informed the head of the convent in no uncertain terms that she was to dispose of the donkey immediately. So she found a neighboring farmer who was willing to buy the animal for ten dollars. The paper carried the story: "NUN PEDDLES ASS FOR TEN BUCKS."

They buried the bishop the next day.

•

How do we know that Adam and Eve were Irish?

Because Adam looked down at Eve and said, "Oh, hair," and Eve looked down at Adam and said, "Oh, tool!

•

The Pope finally got a moment to himself and was masturbating furiously in the Vatican gardens, when who should come around the hedge but a Japanese tourist. Of course he was loaded down with the usual photographic paraphernalia, and before the Pope could zip up his fly the tourist had gotten off a couple of shots.

Panicked, the Pope walked over and complimented the Japanese man on his fine equipment. "I've always wanted a camera like that," he lied desperately. "Would you take fifteen thousand for it?"

The Japanese tourist bowed deeply, took the cash, handed over the Nikon, and left the garden smiling.

On his way back to his chambers the Pope had the bad luck to run into one of his cardinals who was something of a photographer himself. "Nice camera," he complimented the Pope. "Where'd you get it?"

"Actually, from a native of Japan," answered the Pope.

"Very clever; what did you pay for it?" quizzed the Cardinal.

"Fifteen thousand dollars," blurted the Pope.

"Mother of God! He must have seen you coming!"

•

Mad Max, a skinhead punk rocker, started dating a nun, and he really liked her a lot. One night they ended up at his apartment after a particularly pleasant evening of dining and dancing. But when he asked her to go to bed with him, she explained that she was saving herself for God.

A week or so later they ended up at his apartment again, but again her answer was that she was saving herself for God. Understandably, the skinhead was depressed, and on the bus the next morning he confided in the nice lady bus driver.

On learning the nun's name, the bus driver frowned and gave the matter some serious thought. "Sister Mary, eh," he said. "You know, I've heard that Sister Mary goes to the cemetery to pray every night. Why don't you buy a white beard and wig and drape yourself in a sheet and tell her you're God?"

Mad Max figured it was worth a try. All dressed up, he came across the nun in the graveyard and said in a booming voice, "I am God. Let's do it."

Sister Mary looked up from her prayers. "Oh, My Lord," she said, "if it's really You . . ." and proceeded to open her habit. Not until they were going at it hot and heavy did the guy rip his wig and beard off and shout, "Mad Max!"

So she ripped off her wimple and yelled, "Bus driver!"

•

Are you aware that it wasn't an apple that caused the problems in the Garden of Eden?

It was the pair on the ground.

•

Old Timothy O'Day was clearly on his deathbed. So his son, Liam, was completely taken aback when the old man plucked at his sleeve, drew him close, and said, "My boy, it's time for you to go for the Protestant minister."

"But Dad," gasped Liam, "what on earth would a good Catholic like yourself be wanting with a minister at a time like this—meaning no disrespect, of course."

"Get the minister," ordered O'Day fiercely, and after a few more sputtering protests, his son hurried off to honor what might be his father's last request. He was back with the Reverend Wilson within forty-five minutes, and listened in dismay outside the door as the minister converted his father and administered the Protestant last rites.

His distress, however, paled beside that of Father McGuire, who hurried up the stairs past the departing Reverend Wilson. "Tim, Tim, *why*?" he cried, bursting into the old man's room. "We went to St. Joseph's together. We were altar boys at Our Lady of the Sacred Heart. I was there at your First Communion and you saw the first Mass I performed. How in the world could you do such a thing?"

"Paddy," said old O'Day, leaning back against his pillows, "I figured if somebody had to go, better one of them than one of us."

•

When the Mother Superior answered the knock at the convent door, she found two leprechauns shuffling their feet on the doorsill. "Aye an' begorrah, Mother Superior," said the foremost one after an awkward pause, "would ye be havin' any leprechaun nuns in your church?"

The nun shook her head solemnly.

The little man shuffled his feet a bit more, then piped up,

"An' would there be any leprechaun nuns in the convent?"

"No, my boys," said the Mother Superior gravely.

"Ye see, laddy," cried the leprechaun, whirling around to his companion triumphantly. "I *told* you ye been fuckin' a penguin!"

.

Why is the pope against abortion?

He doesn't want Catholics to have any misconceptions.

.

Why is the Catholic Church hiring hundreds of blacks?

To teach the congregation the rhythm method.

.

Getting ready to pray with his wife, a minister noticed that she was already in bed. "Why, my dear," he said, "you shouldn't be in bed, you should be on your knees."

"Could we hold off tonight, honey?" the wife asked. "My throat hurts."

.

Things were a little slow in heaven one evening, so Moses suggested to Jesus that they go down to earth and visit a whorehouse.

"You go first, Jesus," Moses said, as he settled down in the waiting room with a magazine.

To Moses's amazement, Jesus walked out of the bedroom thirty seconds later. "Boy, that was fast," he commented.

"I'm such a jerk," Jesus replied in disgust. "The woman opened her legs and showed me her hole, but before I could stop myself, I healed the damned thing closed."

.

Did you hear about the new Cabbage Patch Dolls for atheists' kids?

They're stuffed with catnip and dressed as early Christians.

•

When a live sex show opened up on Main Street, the town's clergymen formed a delegation to check out the show and determine its risk to their congregations. Coming out of the theater, they all agreed that it was truly a terrible show, miserable even as entertainment. Suddenly the Episcopal minister stopped, saying, "I have to go back in—I forgot my hat."

"No you didn't," pointed out the priest. "It's hanging on your lap."

•

First drunk: "I'm Jesus Christ."

Second drunk: "Naw—you're just a bum like me."

First drunk: "Come with me and I'll prove it." (He knocks on the whorehouse door.)

Madam (opening the door): "Jesus Christ! Are you here again?"

•

An angry crowd was milling around Jesus as he began his ascent up the hill to Calvary, and he got nervous when he saw them picking up rocks from the pathway. Raising his hands, Jesus intoned, "Let he who is without sin cast the first stone."

A hush fell over the crowd. Then—thunk!—a rock hit him on the temple. "Ma," said Jesus, flinching, "you always were a bitch."

•

When the golfer went to retrieve his ball from deep in the woods, he was startled to come across a witch stirring a huge cauldron. Observing the steaming green brew with fascination, he finally asked, "What's in there?"

"A magic brew," hissed the witch. "One swig and you'll play better golf than anyone in the world. You'll be unbeatable."

"Fantastic!" exclaimed the golfer, his eyes lighting up. "Let me have some."

"Hold your horses," cackled the hag gleefully. "There's a catch. You'll pay for it with your sex life: it'll become the worst in the world."

The man stopped to think it over. "No sex . . . great golf . . ." he mused. "Give me a cup."

Finding his ball, the golfer headed out of the woods, finished his game in no time, and went on to whip the club champion that afternoon. Soon he became the best golfer in the country, constantly on tour, but a year later he found himself on the same course. Out of curiosity he went back into the woods, and sure enough the witch was still there, stirring her brew. "You again," she wheezed, looking up blearily. "How's your golf game?"

He recited his latest triumphs on the circuit.

"And your sex life?" The witch tittered malevolently, but her expression changed to surprise when he answered, "Not bad."

"Not bad? How many times have you gotten laid this year?" The witch's curiosity had clearly gotten the best of her.

"Three, maybe four times," answered the golfer.

"And you call that 'not bad'?" retorted the witch.

"Actually, no," said the golfer modestly, "not for a Catholic priest with a very small congregation."

MISCELLANEOUS

A trio of musicians was accorded the great honor of being invited to play before the crowned heads of Europe, and when they returned to America, the piccolo player told the following story:

"We played for the King of Spain and he liked our music so much that after the concert he instructed his treasurer to fill our instruments with gold. There was my friend with the French horn full of gold and my friend with the saxophone full of gold and there I was with that goddamned piccolo.

"Then we went on to Paris, and the King of France was so well entertained that he ordered our instruments filled with precious stones. So there was my friend with the French horn full of jewels and my friend with the sax full of jewels and there I was with that goddamned piccolo.

"Our last concert was for the Austro-Hungarian Emperor and our music was not to his liking at all. So much so that he instructed his guard to take us out and shove our instruments up our asses. So there was my friend with his French horn, my friend with his sax . . . and there I was with my *goddamned piccolo*."

•

Which would you rather be: a witch, a wizard, or a whale?
—if you're a witch, you have a hollow weenie;
—if you're a wizard, you have crystal balls;
—and if you're a whale, you have a Moby Dick.

•

What do you call a horny pumpkin?
—an ejack-o-lantern.

•

What's the definition of skyjacking?
—a hand job at 32,000 feet.

•

What gets wetter as it dries?
—toilet paper.

•

What's the ultimate in punk?
—a pubic mohawk.

•

What's Jell-O?
—Kool-Aid with a hard-on.

•

How do you drive away from an orange?
—Peel out!

•

So how do you sneak up on celery?
—Stalk.

•

What's the difference between a plane and a baby?
—A plane goes from city to city, and a baby goes from titty to titty.

•

How many surrealists does it take to change a light bulb?
—Potato.

•

What do sex and bridge have in common?
—If you don't have a good partner, a good hand will do.

•

What's the difference between an asshole and a rectum?
—You can't put your arm around a rectum. [Use accompanying gesture.]

•

A young maiden was much enamored of a certain fellow. After a respectable amount of time had passed, she could contain herself no longer and shyly offered him her honor. The young man honored her offer, and that's the way it went all night: honor and offer, honor and offer . . .

•

What do you call a Russian in a whorehouse?
—a Cummunist.

•

Mrs. Fisher, the sixth-grade teacher, tells the class that today they're going to have a spelling bee. Instructing the first kid to stand up, she asks, "Robert, what does your father do for a living? Say it nice and clearly, and then spell it out."

"My father's a baker," answers Robert. "B-A-K-E-R-R."

"That's not quite right, Robert. Try again," chides Mrs. Fisher gently.

"B-A—" says Robert, thinking hard, "K-E-R."

"Very good. Now, Cecily?"

"Doctor. D-O-C-T-O-R." Cecily sits down smugly.

"Very good. Herbie?"

Herbie stands up and says, "Shiplayer. S-H-I-T—"

"No, Herbie," interrupts Mrs. Fisher. "Try again."

"Ship . . . layer. S-H-I-T—"

"No, no, no. Go to the blackboard and write it out and you'll see your mistake."

As Herbie heads toward the front of the class, Mrs. Fisher turns to the next child, Lenny, who jumps up and says, "My father's a bookie. That's B-double O-K-I-E and I'll lay you six to one that dope puts 'shit' on the board."

•

What do you get when you walk through Central Park with $1000 in your pocket?
    —mugged.

•

A woman was sitting next to a stranger in a bar when a disgusting smell came through the air. "Did you shit in your pants?" she asked disgustedly, turning to her neighbor.

"Sure did," was the reply.

"Well be a gentleman and go clean yourself!" she retorted, shocked.

"You gotta point, but let me finish first."

•

A couple of new sayings from Confucius:
 —he who stands on toilet seat is high on pot; and,
 —he who sniffs Coke, drowns.

•

If you're an American when you go into the bathroom and an American when you come out, what are you while you're in the bathroom?
 European.

•

[Instruct subject to twirl one finger in air while joke is being told.]
 Say, "Knock, knock."
 Subject: "Who's there?"
 Say, "Yah," and wait.

•

What's toilet paper?
 Film for your brownie.

•

What's LXIX?
 Sixty-nine the hard way.

•

Mrs. Lewis wanted to redecorate the bedroom to surprise her husband, so she arranged for the painter to come while her husband was at work, and to finish the job in one day. When her husband got home she proudly showed him the room, and he loved it. Unfortunately he didn't realize the paint was still wet, and when he leaned back he left a big blotch against the wall.
 "Don't worry about it, honey," reassured the wife. "I'll

take care of it." The next morning Mrs. Lewis called up to make a final request of the painter. "Come see where my husband put his hand last night."

"No thanks, lady," answered the painter. "I'll settle for a cup of coffee."

•

What's the difference between McDonalds and a New York prostitute?

McDonalds has served only fifty billion.

•

The third-grade teacher was shocked to find words like *cock, cunt,* and *asshole* scrawled on the blackboard when she walked into the classroom. "Children," she said sternly, "you are much too young to use such vile language. Now we're all going to close our eyes and count to fifty, and while we're counting I want the little boy or girl who wrote those words to tiptoe up and erase them."

At the signal, the teacher and her students closed their eyes and the teacher counted out loud, very slowly. When she reached fifty, she said, "All right, class, everybody open their eyes."

All eyes went to the blackboard.

None of the words had been erased, and below them was the message: "Fuck you, teacher. The Phantom strikes again."

•

Two Scotsmen were avid golfers and had played together every Thursday for many years. The sixth tee was near the road that led to the local cemetery.

One day as they reached that particular tee a funeral passed by, and old Hamish turned and raised his club in salute.

"Mon," exclaimed Hector, "in all these years we've been

a playing this course, and that's the first time I've seen ye paying any respect for the dead."

"Aye, weel," explained Hamish, "when you have been married to a woman for forty years, she's entitled to a wee bit of respect."

•

This man drove up to a large puddle in his brand-new Mercedes. There was a man standing right next to it, so the driver leaned out and asked if the puddle was shallow. Receiving an affirmative, the man drove on, only to have his car sink slowly out of sight into the puddle. Sputtering with rage, the driver strode over to the bystander and demanded, "Why the hell did you tell me it was shallow enough to drive right through?"

"I don't understand it," said the man, scratching his head in puzzlement. "It only came up to here [see visual] on those ducks."

•

Tired and hungry, three men came across a farm as night fell, and asked the farmer if they might spend the night. The farmer gave them permission, but explained that as he had nothing very grand to offer in the way of lodgings, one man would have to sleep with the cows, the second in with the vegetables, and the third with his eighteen daughters.

The next morning as they started out on the road again, the three travelers compared notes on the night they had spent. "To tell the truth," muttered the first one, "I feel like a cow, and I smell like one."

The second said he smelled like potatoes, and suspected he looked like one. "And how about you?" he asked of the third man.

"Me? I feel like a golf course."

•

"Shay, what're these for?" asked the drunk, noticing three darts sitting on the bar.

"See the dartboard over there?" The bartender waved toward a dark corner. "Anybody that gets three bulls-eyes in a row wins a prize."

"Okay," said the drunk, "think I'll give it a shot." Steadying himself with one hand, he tossed the first dart, and to the bartender's amazement it landed dead center. He was swaying so much he could barely pick up the second dart and face the right direction, but it too landed in the center. And after the third throw his head hit the bar with a loud thump, but not before it was clear that he had miraculously thrown three bulls-eyes in a row. Getting unsteadily to his feet, the drunk demanded his prize.

"No problem pal, just hold your horses," soothed the astonished bartender, wondering what the hell to do. No one had ever gotten this far before. Suddenly inspired, he went over to the aquarium behind the bar, fished out a turtle, and handed it to the drunk. "Here's your prize!" he said brightly.

The drunk's red-nosed face lit up. "Hey, thanks a lot," he said, pocketed the turtle, and staggered out into the street.

A few weeks later the same guy lurched in, made his way to a barstool, and shouted, "Lemme try for another prize!"

"Sure," said the bartender confidently, handing him the darts. And to the bartender's utter amazement the drunk managed to repeat his amazing feat, though this time he passed out cold on the floor after the third throw. Coming to, he struggled to his feet and demanded his prize.

"Uh . . . okay," mumbled the flabbergasted bartender, "but I gotta tell you, you're the first guy to manage this twice, and I don't know what the hell to give you. What'd you get last time?"

After a prodigious belch, a smile came over the drunk's face. "Roast beef on a hard roll."

•

The second grade's afternoon discussion was about what the children's daddies did for a living. "Mikey, you go first," coaxed Miss Ferguson.

Mikey stood up and said, "My daddy works in the First National Bank."

"Thank you, Mikey. Kelsey, what about your daddy?"

"My father sells insurance," answered the little girl.

"Very good, Kelsey. Joseph?"

Joseph stood up and announced, "My father plays the piano in a whorehouse."

Blushing beet-red, Miss Ferguson quickly changed the subject to geography, but that afternoon she walked Joseph home. "Can I help you?" asked Joseph's father when he answered the door.

"Your son Joseph is my student, and today he told the entire class you play piano in a whorehouse," reported the teacher indignantly. "I'd like the truth of the matter, please."

"Oh, actually I'm an attorney," said the boy's father nonchalantly, "but you can't tell *that* to a seven-year-old."

•

How many actors does it take to change a light bulb?

One hundred. One to change the bulb, and ninety-nine to say, "I could have done that."

•

A rather scruffy-looking type came into a bank. Reaching the head of the line, he said to the teller, "I wanna open a fucking checking account."

111

"Certainly, sir," answered the teller, "but there's no need to use that kind of language."

"Couldja move it along lady? I just wanna open a fucking checking account," growled the would-be customer.

"I'll be glad to be of service, sir," said the teller, flushing slightly, "but I would appreciate not being spoken to in that way."

"Just lemme open a fucking checking account, okay?"

"I'm afraid I'm going to have to speak to the branch manager," said the flustered teller, slipping off her stool and returning shortly with a dapper middle-aged man who asked how he could be of service.

"I just won the ten-million-dollar lottery," snarled the man, "and all I wanna do is open a fucking checking account."

"I see," said the manager sympathetically. "And this bitch is giving you trouble?"

•

"I'm afraid I have to operate immediately," pronounced the doctor gravely.

"But, Doctor, this was just a routine check-up," protested the patient. "I feel terrific!"

"That just goes to show why check-ups are such a good idea," explained the doctor. "This condition might have killed you. Even as is, it's going to be a long and difficult operation, and it's going to cost you thirty thousand dollars."

The patient paled. "I don't have that kind of money, doc," he protested weakly.

"That's okay," said the doctor soothingly, "it doesn't have to be paid in full. We can arrange a monthly installment plan."

"Oh, I see . . . Sort of like buying a car?"

"Yeah," said the doctor, "I am."

•

How did the shrink greet his fellow psychiatrist when they met on the street?

"You're fine—how am I?"

•

How can a bartender tell which men like Moose Head?

By looking for the ones with antler marks on their lips.

•

"Do you smoke after sex?" asked the horny woman of the Martian visitor.

"I don't know," confessed the Martian after considering the question for a minute. "I never looked."

•

A shipwrecked man had spent ten years alone on a desert island, so he was overjoyed when a woman washed ashore one day. Tattered and clutching only a small watertight bag, she was the sole survivor of the wreck of a pleasure boat on the island's coral reef. The man could hardly wait to tell her of his survival by his wits alone for all that time.

"You mean you've been marooned for *ten* years?" asked the woman, awestruck.

"That's right," said the man, hanging his head modestly.

"Say, did you used to smoke?"

"You bet. Why?"

"I'd be delighted to offer you your first cigarette in ten years." With a smile, the woman pulled one out of her bag.

"Wow! Thanks a lot," said the man, taking a grateful puff.

"You didn't happen to be a drinking man, did you?" asked the woman shyly.

"I've been known to enjoy a glass or two," the man confessed, blowing smoke rings happily.

"Well, here you go," she said, pulling a flask out of her bag. As the man was gratefully taking a swig, the woman blushed. "Gee, I just realized it's been ten years since you, uh, played around, right?"

"Don't tell me," said the guy, a look of ecstasy coming over his face. "Have you got a set of *golf clubs* in that bag?"

•

Did you hear about the tight end who was sentenced to a prison term?

He came out a wide receiver.

•

What's the difference between spinach and boogers?

Not everyone likes the taste of spinach.

•

A Wyoming cowhand went to Denver for a little R&R, but didn't succeed in coping too well with the complexities of city life. In fact, midnight found him alone in his hotel room, jerking off.

Suddenly the door was opened by a bellhop carrying a drink intended for the room next door. "Pardon me, sir," said the flustered bellhop, "but where would you like me to set down your drink?"

"I didn't order a drink," retorted the cowhand, thinking fast. "Can't you see I'm already so drunk that I'm taking advantage of me?"

•

"Think times are hard now?" croaked the old geezer to his son-in-law. "Why I remember a cold winter during the Depression, back in '32, when the prostitutes would give you a free blow job just to get something warm in their stomachs . . ."

•

Two none-too-bright ranch hands went into Sacramento for a wild night. They took two obliging hookers back to their hotel room, where things proceeded to heat up. At this point the girls provided them with condoms, explaining that they were protection against AIDS, VD, and herpes.

A couple of hours after the girls had left, one ranch hand poked the other. "Sal," he asked sleepily, "do you really care if those girls get VD?"

"Naw," Jake mumbled.

"So let's take these damn things off—I have to take a wicked piss!"

•

Then there was Jake and Sal's fishing expedition. Sal went ahead to set up camp, only to realize that the rocky shores around Jackson Hole would make it impossible to maneuver their big boat to the water. Hiking into the nearest town, he sent his buddy a telegram instructing him to bring punts and a canoe instead.

Two days later, right on schedule, Jake arrived with two girls in tow. "I didn't know what a panoe was," he explained cheerfully, "but I got the girls."

•

What's the problem with dating an ex-smoker?

He'll need something to do with his hands.

•

It was time for the second grade to discuss what their daddies did for a living. First Miss Wilcox called on Annie, who stood up and said, "My Daddy's a fireman."

"Very good, Annie. Jimmy, what does your father do?"

"He's a policeman," said the little boy proudly.

"That's a fine profession," commented the teacher. "How about your daddy, Archie?"

"He eats light bulbs."

"What?" blurted Miss Wilcox. "Your father eats light bulbs?"

"Yeah," said the snot-nosed kid defensively.

"Archie, whatever makes you think that's what he does?" asked the teacher kindly.

"Well," Archie explained, "last night when I was walking past my parents' bedroom I heard my dad say, "Hey, baby, turn out the light and I'll eat it.""

•

The obstetrician was surprised when the husband of one of his patients requested an appointment. When the time came he ushered him into his office and asked, "What can I do for you?"

"Doc," confessed the husband, "I'm worried because our new baby has red hair."

"Why is that a cause for concern?" asked the doctor.

"Well, I have black hair, my wife has black hair, and all four grandparents have black hair."

The doctor thought for a minute or two. "How often do you and your wife have sex?" he asked.

"About twice a year," answered the worried husband.

"That explains it," proclaimed the obstetrician. "The red hair is rust."

TOO TASTELESS TO BE INCLUDED

Why are there nude photographs of black women?
  So that apes can masturbate.

•

After entertaining her boyfriend, a young lady was too lazy to get out of bed and dispose of the rubber, so she threw it out the window. Looking out, she was horrified to see that a six-year-old boy had picked it up.

"Say, sonny," she stammered, pulling on her robe and leaning out the window, "I'll give you ten dollars for that . . . uh . . . that Twinkie!"

"You got a deal, lady!" said the little boy happily.

"Mommy, guess what?" he shouted as soon as he got in his front door. "I got ten dollars for a Twinkie, and I'd already eaten the cream out of the middle!"

•

Why do blacks have such thick lips?
  So they can unclog toilets.

•

What's a naked Polish girl doing when she bends over?
  Applying for a job.

•

> Little Jack Horner sat in a corner
> Eating his girlfriend dry.
> He stuck in his tongue,
> Pulled out some come,
> And said, "This is a great piece of pie!"

•

"Daddy, Daddy, I don't want to play Ferris wheel any-more—"
  "Shut up so I can get it in more."

•

"Mommy, Mommy, I don't want to eat by candlelight—"
  "Shut up or I'll scrape the wax out of your other ear."

•

"Mommy, Mommy, I hate olives—"
  "Shut up or I'll scrape your other eye out."

•

When his girlfriend died suddenly, Jimmy was truly dis-traught. When the truck came to take her off to the morgue, he pulled the attendant aside and asked if he could pay a final visit to his beloved.
  "Sure," said the guy, but indicated it would cost him.

Jimmy readily agreed, handed over the money at the morgue, and was shown to the room where her corpse lay on an autopsy table. "God, I'd really like to kiss her one more time," he admitted wistfully. The attendant named a price, and though he was getting short on cash, Jimmy readily handed it over.

After the kiss, Jimmy looked up with tears in his eyes and confessed that he still found her incredibly attractive, so much so that he desperately wanted to do it with her one more time.

Nervous about someone coming in, the attendant was reluctant to give in to Jimmy's last request. Finally they agreed that in return for the last of Jimmy's cash, he would cut out the relevant part of the woman's anatomy and let Jimmy take it home. Finishing the job, the attendant turned to Jimmy and asked if he'd like it wrapped up.

"No, thank you," answered Jimmy. "I'll eat it here."

•

What should you do if your toddler swallows a golf ball?
Feed him Ex-Lax and hold him over the green.

•

Jack was checking out of the fleabag motel when the owner sheepishly acknowledged that the place had been having a bit of a problem with flies lately. "Did they disturb your sleep last night, sir?" he inquired politely.

"Nah," replied Jack. "I bunched 'em up—I shat in the corner."

•

Why do innocent boys have wet dreams?
Because Jesus sucks.

•

When the doctor answered his phone, a frantic father was on the other end. "Come quick, Doc, my little boy just swallowed a rubber!"

The doctor hung up, grabbed his bag, and was running for the door when the phone rang again.

"Never mind, Doc," said the boy's father. "I found another one."

•

What's grosser than gross?

Popping a boner and running out of skin.

•

There once was a lady named Dot
Who lived off of pig shit and snot.
  When she couldn't get these
  She ate the green cheese
That she scraped off the sides of her twat.

•

What's the definition of relative humidity?

The sweat on your balls when you're fucking your sister.

Would you like to see your favorite tasteless jokes in print? If so, send them to:

Blanche Knott
% St. Martin's Press
175 Fifth Avenue
New York, N.Y. 10010

Remember, we're sorry, but no compensation or credit can be given. But we *love* hearing from our tasteless readers.

35

What do you call a series of books that will have you groaning with laughter?

Blanche Knott's
Truly Tasteless Jokes

Over 3 million copies of Truly Tasteless Jokes in print!

TRULY TASTELESS JOKES IV
_____ 90365-0 $2.95 U.S.   _____ 90366-9 $3.50 Can.

TRULY TASTELESS JOKES V
_____ 90371-5 $2.95 U.S.   _____ 90372-3 $3.50 Can.

TRULY TASTELESS JOKES VI
_____ 90361-8 $2.95 U.S.   _____ 90373-1 $3.75 Can.

THE TRULY TASTELESS JOKE-A-DATE BOOK 1987
Spiral bound for easy access to a laugh a day!
_____ 90485-1 $3.95 U.S.   _____ 90523-8 $4.95 Can.

BLANCHE KNOTT'S BOOK OF TRULY TASTELESS ETIQUETTE
Bad taste for *all* occasions!
_____ 90590-4 $3.50 U.S.   _____ 90591-2 $4.50 Can.

ST. MARTIN'S PRESS—MAIL SALES
175 Fifth Avenue, New York, NY 10010

Please send me the book(s) I have checked above. I am enclosing a check or money order (not cash) for $_____ plus 75¢ per order to cover postage and handling (New York residents add applicable sales tax).

Name _____

Address _____

City _____ State_____ Zip Code_____
Allow at least 4 to 6 weeks for delivery   34